JONAH
SPEAKS
AGAIN

S0-ATO-231

JONAH SPEAKS AGAIN

A DISCUSSION GUIDE
ON THE BOOK OF JONAH

DON W. HILLIS

BAKER BOOK HOUSE
Grand Rapids, Michigan

Library of Congress Catalog Card Number: 67-18180

Copyright, 1967, 1973 by
Baker Book House Company
ISBN: 0-8010-4096-5

Formerly published under the title: *The Book of Jonah, A Study Manual*

Printed in the
United States of America

24.9207
H559

LIFE Pacific College
Alumni Library
1100 West Covina Blvd.
San Dimas, CA 91773

DEDICATED TO
the missionaries of
The Evangelical Alliance Mission in particular
and to all servants of the Lord in general,
with the prayer
that God will enable each one
to minister
with faith and courage
in the Nineveh to which God has sent him.

Life Pacific College
Alumni Library
1100 West Covina Blvd
San Dimas, CA 91773

CONTENTS

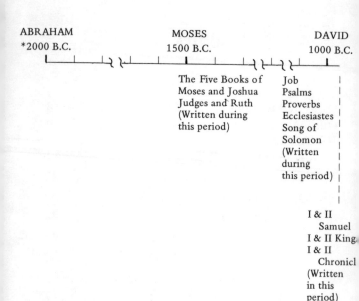

ABRAHAM
*2000 B.C.

MOSES
1500 B.C.

DAVID
1000 B.C.

The Five Books of
Moses and Joshua
Judges and Ruth
(Written during
this period)

Job
Psalms
Proverbs
Ecclesiastes
Song of
Solomon
(Written
during
this period)

I & II
Samuel
I & II King.
I & II
Chronicl
(Written
in this
period)

1. The division of Israel into two kingdoms took place about 900 B.C.
2. Note that Jonah appeared on the scene of history about 800 B.C.
3. The Assyrian Empire ruled the world from 900 B.C. to 600 B.C.
4. The northern kingdom of Israel was already paying tribute to Assyria when Jonah came on the scene. Jonah knew that the Assyrian Empire was the vessel in God's hand, chosen to scourge Israel.

HISTORICAL PERSPECTIVE

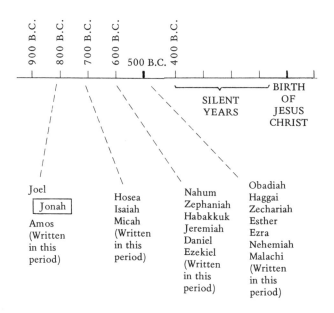

| 900 B.C. | 800 B.C. | 700 B.C. | 600 B.C. | 500 B.C. | 400 B.C. |

SILENT YEARS

BIRTH OF JESUS CHRIST

Joel

Jonah

Amos
(Written
in this
period)

Hosea
Isaiah
Micah
(Written
in this
period)

Nahum
Zephaniah
Habakkuk
Jeremiah
Daniel
Ezekiel
(Written
in this
period)

Obadiah
Haggai
Zechariah
Esther
Ezra
Nehemiah
Malachi
(Written
in this
period)

5. The northern kingdom was finally taken into captivity, its capital city of Samaria destroyed and its people killed or dispersed about 700 B.C.
6. Israel's southern kingdom (Judah) was invaded by the Assyrians several times after Samaria's destruction.
7. The back of Assyrian power was finally broken by the Medes and Babylonians about 600 B.C.

*Because various chronologists differ slightly in the dates they give we have retained round numbers in this chart.

SUGGESTED READING

COMMENTARIES

Matthew Henry—Revell
Clarke's   Commentary—Abingdon-Cokesbury
Expositor's Bible—Eerdmans
Lange's Commentary—Zondervan
Wycliffe Bible Commentary—Moody
Layman's Handy Commentary—Zondervan

BOOKS

Unger's Bible Handbook—Moody
The Twelve Minor Prophets, by G. L. Robinson—Baker
The Servant and the Dove, by Gaebelein—Our Hope
The Minor Prophets, by E. B. Pusey—Baker
Jonah Fact or Fiction, by DeHaan—Zondervan
The City and the Sign, by G. Bull—Baker
A Commentary on the Minor Prophets, by H. Hailey—Baker
The Minor Prophets, by J. P. Lewis—Baker
Halley's Bible Handbook—Zondervan
Living Prophecies, by Taylor—Tyndale House
Whyte's Bible Characters (Vol. I)—Zondervan
The Minor Prophets, by G. C. Morgan—Revell
An Introduction to the Old Testament, by E. J. Young—Eerdmans

THE BOOK OF JONAH

GENERAL OUTLINE

DETAILED OUTLINE

JONAH SPEAKS—

1   With Authority

Few books in the Old Testament have been the object of more abuse than the four-chapter, forty-eight verse Book of Jonah. Though some of this abuse has come from the sophisticated circles of higher criticism, much of it has come from baser sources. Scoffers have vented their spleens against it while soapbox orators and agnostics have ridiculed this "fish story."

Others have written the Book of Jonah off as a myth, parable, or an allegory. Not believing in the inspiration of the Scriptures, they have been content to give it a place in the canon of Holy Writ only because the book contains spiritual lessons which are applicable to us even though the book itself is only a myth.

There have, on the other hand, always been a great many Jewish and Christian scholars who have approved the place given to the Book of Jonah in the Scriptures. This claim can also be made with reference to the vast majority of lay readers among both groups.

The following seven facts will help us understand why this is true. We will discover in them that Jonah does indeed speak with authority.

1. *There seems to be no significant reason why Jonah should not be given a place in the canon of Scripture.* Having said this, it must be noted that the majority of those who reject the book apparently do so because they object to the miracles found therein. It will be well, therefore, to list the miracles in order that we might look at them objectively.

1. The sudden heavy wind and raging sea (Chapter 1:4).
2. The immediate cessation of the storm (Chapter 1:15).[1]
3. The prepared sea monster (fish) which was at the right place at the right time to swallow Jonah (Chapter 1:17).
4. Jonah's deliverance from the sea monster (Chapter 2:10).
5. The God-prepared gourd or vine (Chapter 4:6).
6. The God-prepared worm (worms) (Chapter 4:7).
7. A scorching eastwind (Chapter 4:8).

It is noteworthy that most of these miracles can be matched with parallel Bible miracles. For example, miracles 1, 2, and 7 all involve the wind, the sea and the sun. God manipulated these elements to fulfill His purpose. This compares favorably with God's dealings with the wind and the sea at the time His people crossed

---

[1] The lot falling on Jonah was also a miracle. Jonah 1:7. It was a definite intervention of God. Note Proverbs 16:33.

the Red Sea and later when they crossed the Jordan. They also closely parallel our Lord's stilling of the terrifying storm on the Sea of Galilee by His spoken word. Strange it would be if the Creator of the elements, the wind and the water, the sun, the moon and the stars, could not control them.

Miracles 3 and 4 have to do with the obedience of a God-prepared sea monster. If one rejects this miracle, then what is he to do with the story of the thousands of quail which flew into Israel's camp in the wilderness, or of the lowing cattle which left their calves and carried the ark of the covenant back to Israel? What is one to do with Balaam's talking ass, or of the New Testament fish with money in its mouth, or even the multitude of fish which were caught by simply casting the net on the other side of the boat? God's control over and use of His creatures should not surprise us.

Miracles 5 and 6 present the picture of a God-prepared vine and a God-prepared worm. It is possible that the word *worm* here refers more accurately to a species of worm rather than a single worm. It is quite common for a person to refer to his garden being destroyed by a worm when he is not referring to a single worm but to a species of worm. Be that as it may, any rejection of this account would certainly necessitate a rejection of the account of the plagues which fell on Egypt. The lice, the flies, the frogs, etc., all swarmed over Egypt at the will and direction of Almighty God. To suggest that creatures of God cannot be brought under His control is no less than absurd. The Bible consistently assumes God's authority over all things.

If, therefore, we reject the Book of Jonah because of the miracles recorded therein, we must also reject the rest of the Bible. Furthermore, the most significant miracle recorded in the Book of Jonah is the repentance of Nineveh's people. All the other miracles are secondary to this one. Nor do those who have experienced the miracle of conversion in their own lives find it difficult to accept any of the miracles of Jonah including the account of Nineveh's repentance.

2. *There is irrefutable evidence that Jonah was a Jewish prophet of the day in which he wrote.* His identity can be fixed. In II Kings 14:25, we are told concerning Jeroboam, the king of Israel, that "He restored the coast of Israel from the entering of Hamath unto the sea of the plain, according to the word of the Lord God of Israel, which he spake by the hand of his servant, Jonah, the son of Amittai, the prophet, which was of Gath-hepher."

The location of Gath-hepher in Galilee is well known. Furthermore, the traditional tomb of Jonah is located about two miles from Siphhoris just north of Nazareth in Galilee. The road which runs from Nazareth to Tiberius passes near it. It is acknowledged by Jews, Christians, and Moslems.

3. *The cities of Nineveh, Tarshish, and Joppa were historical and geographical facts of Jonah's*

day. Nineveh was the capital of the Assyrian kingdom. It was located on the eastern banks of the Tigris River about 250 miles north of the city of Babylon. More will be said about this city in a later chapter.

Joppa, which today exists under the name of Jaffa, is located north and west of Jerusalem, a few miles south of Caesarea. It is Jerusalem's seaport to the Mediterranean.

Though there was more than one Tarshish in the days of Jonah, it is the consensus of most Bible students that the one referred to in the Book of Jonah was located near the straits of Gibralter on the south coast of Spain. The Book of Jonah does not go into detail with regard to a description of these cities. Obviously, the author assumed his readers would be familiar with them.

4. *There is a simple sincerity about the narration which strongly argues against fraud.* Jonah openly admits his weaknesses. He frankly confesses his disobedience, bigotry and bitterness. This would not be characteristic of an author who was deliberately trying to deceive his readers.

To those who may argue that fraud can be seen in the fact that the author has quoted from some psalms which may have been written after Jonah's day, the question can be reasonably asked, "Did Jonah quote from the psalms or did the psalmist quote from Jonah?" Nor is there conclusive proof that the psalms "quoted" were written after Jonah's day.

5. *The Jew, the Christian, and the Moslem venerate Jonah as a prophet of God.* Though there has been sufficient time for any or all three of these great religious systems to reject the book and expose it as fraud, it has not been done. This speaks rather forcibly for the veracity of the account.[2]

6. *Jesus Christ placed His seal of approval upon the prophet Jonah.* The record of this is given in Luke 11:29-32 as well as in Matthew 12:38-42 and 16:4. We will look at this latter account.

"Then certain of the scribes and of the Pharisees answered, saying, Master, we would see a sign from thee. But he answered and said unto them, An evil and adulterous generation seeketh after a sign; and there shall no sign be given to it, but the sign of the prophet Jonas: For as Jonas was three days and three nights in the whale's belly; so shall the Son of man be three days and three nights in the heart of the earth. The men of Nineveh shall rise in judgment with this generation, and shall condemn it: because they repented at the preaching of Jonas: and, behold, a greater than Jonas is here. The queen of the south shall rise up in the judgment with this generation, and shall condemn it: for she came from the uttermost parts of the earth to hear the wisdom of Solomon; and, behold, a greater than Solomon is here" (Matt. 12:38-42).

"A wicked and adulterous generation seeketh after a sign; and there shall no sign be given unto it, but the sign of the prophet Jonas. And he left them, and departed" (Matt. 16:4).

---

[2] Jonah is read every year by the Jews on the Day of Atonement—yom kippur.

A bit of background on this passage will be helpful. In chapter 12 of Matthew, we are introduced to a series of conflicts between Jesus and the Pharisees. It all began when the Pharisees saw Jesus' disciples pluck and eat corn on the Sabbath. Jesus' response to their criticism was that they ought to re-read the story of David eating the showbread in the temple. Furthermore, He bluntly informed His critics that "the Son of man is Lord even of the Sabbath." Then Jesus added fuel to the fire by going into the synagogue and healing a man with a lame hand. By this time the Pharisees had become angry enough to "take counsel against him, how they might destroy him."

Jesus then temporarily withdrew from the Pharisees and carried on a brief healing ministry at the close of which He quoted a portion of Isaiah 42. He ended the quotation with the words, "and in his name shall the Gentiles trust." These were fighting words to the Pharisees.

The conflict became more deadly when Jesus healed a man "possessed with a devil." This act of healing caused the people to question, "Is not this the Son of God?" The Pharisees were now in a position where they could not stand idly by. They had to come up with an answer. They did. It was a ludicrous accusation—"This fellow doth not cast out devils but by Beelzebub, the prince of devils."

Jesus' answer to this accusation was razor sharp. He said, "And if Satan cast out Satan, he is divided against himself; how shall then his kingdom stand? And if I by Beelzebub cast out devils, by whom do your children cast them out? . . . But if I cast out devils by the Spirit of God, then the kingdom of God is come unto you." In saying this Jesus informed His listeners that to accuse Him of casting out devils by Beelzebub is blasphemy against the Holy Spirit. This is commonly referred to as the "unforgivable sin." Jesus then topped His accusations against the Pharisees by calling them a "generation of vipers," and by assuring them that in the day of judgment their own words would condemn them.

This was strong language and the Pharisees reacted by insisting that Jesus should show them a sign that would substantiate His claims and authority. The passage previously quoted was His answer to their demands for a sign. That this passage argues without fear of refutation for our Lord's acceptance of Jonah as a fact of history and as a prophet of God goes without saying. By no stretch of the imagination could Jesus have been referring to any other than the Book of Jonah.

Furthermore, He pointed deliberately to the story of Jonah's experience of three days and three nights in the belly of the great fish. He said this was a "sign unto the Ninevites." He related this to His own death and resurrection declaring that as Jonah's experience was a sign to the Ninevites, so His experience would be the only "sign" given to Israel.

Our Lord also placed His stamp of approval on the claim that the wicked, affluent and idolatrous people of Nineveh repented at the preaching of Jonah. In other words, Jesus obviously accepted the whole testimony of the prophet as recorded in the Book of Jonah.

It is noteworthy that Jesus made His resurrection the irrefutable and condemning sign to Israel of His person and authority. He did not point to His power over nature, demons, or even death in someone else. Though His demonstrated authority in all these realms had substantiated His right to be Israel's Messiah, He left it to His own predicted resurrection to provide the ultimate proof that He was God.

It is significant that Jesus did not say, "even as Enoch or Elijah ascended to heaven, so shall the Son of man ascend to heaven." Though the Lord's ascension was important, it was not the "sign." He placed His finger on that Old Testament book which He knew would be greatly abused and then as much as said, "That which happened in that book is a type of that which will happen to me." He then assured His hearers that "a greater than Jonah is here."

And that statement suggests the following interesting contrast between the ministries of Jonah and Jesus.

1. Jonah fled from the will of God.	Jesus delighted in the will of God.
2. Jonah suffered for his own waywardness.	Jesus suffered for the waywardness of others.

3. Jonah had to repent of his own sin.	Jesus never had any sin for which to repent.
4. Jonah preached only the wrath of God.	Jesus preached the wrath of God and the love of God.
5. Jonah saw a spectacular acceptance of his message.	Jesus saw an alarming rejection of His message.
6. Jonah sulked at the sight of many repenting sinners.	Jesus rejoiced at the sight of a single sinner brought to repentance.

And, of course, there is as much contrast between the character of Jonah and Jesus as there is between man and God.[3]

If, therefore, Jesus outspokenly and deliberately put His seal of approval on the Book of Jonah, it argues for the advisability of His people to do the same.

7. *The spiritual impact of the message of this little Book of Jonah upon many generations of people also argues for the veracity of the book.* As any openhearted reader will discover, there is something about the content of the book which reveals a volume of truth complementary to the rest of the Bible. The character of both God and man as seen on the pages of this book harmonize with that seen in other readily accepted portions of Holy Writ. Furthermore, it can be said without equivocation that many thousands of lives have been enriched by the spiritual lessons found there.

As Jesus showed Himself alive after His resurrection by "many infallible proofs," being seen

---

[3] Jonah is certainly not a type of Christ.

by many witnesses, so the Book of Jonah has abundant evidence for its veracity. And there are many witnesses to its meaningfulness and blessing.

LET'S DISCUSS

1. Why is it important to accept the Book of Jonah as an inspired, historically accurate book?

2. What is the significance of Jesus pointing to the "sign of the prophet Jonas" in answer to the Pharisees' request for a sign of Christ's authority?

3. How would you define a miracle? Which miracle described in the Book of Jonah is the hardest for you to understand and accept? Tell why.

4. Do you think there is or can be mass repentance today comparable to that which took place in Nineveh? Why, or why not?

5. Generally speaking, the purpose of most miracles described in the Bible is to lead men to a true faith in God. What would you say to a person who expects a miracle (e.g., healing) for personal reasons only?

6. Jonah lived in a time when his country was enjoying prosperity. How is contemporary American culture similar to that of Israel in Jonah's day? Is a high standard of living a deterrent to true spirituality? How does it affect one's attitudes toward missions?

7. What would you say is the primary lesson of the Book of Jonah?

2 About Prophecy

The Book of Jonah is obviously history. It is the story of a prophet's disobedience and discipline. Why then does it appear among the prophets?

One answer is that Jonah was himself a prophet. But that is inadequate. Elijah and Elisha were prophets of much greater prominence than Jonah and yet their stories appear in the books of history. There must be a more significant reason why Jonah is placed with the prophets. The fact that the Book of Jonah contains one prophetic statement ("yet forty days and Nineveh shall be overthrown"), is hardly sufficient to give it that place. On the contrary, that fact alone would seem sufficient to eliminate it from the prophets.

And yet, there it is—one of the minor prophets. And there is a reason, a good reason for it being there. The entire story of the book is a prophetic picture. In other words, it is prophecy in type. It is as if God were saying to Israel, "Do you want prophetic truth about yourself? Do you want to know how you as a nation will act and what will be the end thereof. Then look at Jonah. He is a prophetic object lesson. His experiences are prophetic of yours."

It was not uncommon for God to call upon His prophets to demonstrate their messages. Jeremiah was commanded to purchase "a linen girdle" (waistband), and bury it until it rotted. This was to illustrate the way in which God would "mar the pride of Judah, and the great pride of Jerusalem" (Jer. 13:9). Hosea was asked to marry an unfaithful wife as an illustration of God's love and faithfulness to Israel in her unfaithfulness. In the Book of Jonah, God dramatizes Israel's future. This is readily seen as we review the salient points of Jonah's experience. Here they are.

1. Jonah was commissioned to be a witness to the Gentiles. He was the only Old Testament prophet so commissioned.
2. Jonah was disobedient to his commission and he endeavored to escape the will of God.
3. Jonah was cast into the sea and suffered severe discipline.
4. Jonah was miraculously preserved (resurrected) and given a second opportunity to witness to the Gentiles.
5. Jonah experienced great response to his final ministry.

A brief review of Israel's history will immediately reveal the way in which it parallels the experience of Jonah.

1. *Like Jonah, Israel was chosen to be a witness to a Gentile world.* The descendants of Abraham were a select people. To them belonged the adoption, the glory, the covenants, the law, the promises and the service of God (Rom. 9:4). Through them all the nations of the earth were to be blessed (Gen. 12:2-3).

As a holy people, they were to be God's witnesses to the whole world. "Ye are my witnesses, saith the Lord, and my servant whom I have chosen: that ye may know and believe me and understand that I am He: before me there was no god formed, neither shall there be after me. I, even I, am the Lord; and beside me there is no saviour. I have declared and have saved, and I have shown when there was no strange god among you. Therefore ye are my witnesses, saith the Lord, that I am God" (Isa. 43:10-12). The descendants of Abraham were to declare God's glory "among the heathen; his marvelous works among all nations" (I Chron. 16:24).

Great were the promises of God to Israel if she would obey His commands. She was to be set "on high above all the nations of the earth" (Deut. 28:1). She was to be blessed in everything she did. And all the people of the earth were to see that "thou art called by the name of the Lord; and they shall be afraid of thee" (Deut. 28:10). Israel was indeed chosen to be a witness to the Gentile world.

2. *Like Jonah, Israel was disobedient to her God-given commission.* Early in Israel's wilder-

ness experience, she turned to idolatry. ". . . the people gathered themselves together unto Aaron, and said unto him, Up, make us gods, which shall go before us. . ." (Exod. 32:1). Later the people complained and even expressed their desire to return to Egypt in order to eat of the leeks, the onions, and the garlic (Num. 11). During the period of the Judges and of the Kings, Israel's witness for God rose and fell like the ocean tide. In the overall picture, her testimony was a failure except for those occasional times when her leaders were used of God to bring revival to the nation. There were times when her behavior was worse than that of the pagan nations around about her. The name of God was often degraded among the heathen as a result of Israel's poor testimony. "For the name of God is blasphemed among the Gentiles through you" (Rom. 2:24).

Israel was indeed disobedient to her God-given commission. Paul quotes Isaiah as saying, "All day long I have stretched forth my hands unto a disobedient and gainsaying people" (Rom. 10:21).

3. *Like Jonah, Israel was cast out.* There are few facts of history more easily documented than the dispersion of the Jewish people. The ten tribes of the Northern Kingdom were taken captive and dispersed about 700 B.C. by the Assyrian armies. The two tribes of the Southern Kingdom were overrun by the Babylonians around 600 B.C. However, some of the people

were allowed to return to Palestine after the seventy-year captivity. Palestine was then swallowed up by the Roman Empire before the days of Christ only to have Jerusalem destroyed and the Jews scattered once again in A.D. 70.

Within two hundred years after David, Israel's spiritual condition had so deteriorated that her few true prophets began predicting her downfall and dispersion. Moses had told them five hundred years before David that this would happen if they did not obey God. "The Lord shall cause thee to be smitten before thine enemies; thou shalt go out one way against them, and flee seven ways, before them; and shalt be removed into all the kingdoms of the earth" (Deut. 28:25).

In Deuteronomy 4:27, we read, "And the Lord shall scatter you among the nations, and ye shall be left few in number among the heathen whither the Lord shall lead you."

"And they shall know that I am the Lord, when I shall scatter them among the nations and disperse them into countries, and the cities that are inhabited shall be laid waste and the land shall be desolate, and ye shall know that I am the Lord," says Ezekiel (12:15, 20).

God's prophetic word to Moses was "And I will make your cities waste and will bring your sanctuaries unto desolation, and I will not smell the savor of your sweet odors. And I will bring the land into desolation, and your enemies which dwell therein shall be astonished at it.

26

And I will scatter you among the heathen, and will draw out a sword after you: and your land shall be desolate and your cities waste" (Lev. 26:31-33).

The fact that Israel as a nation was dispersed abroad, cut off, and cast away cannot be refuted. Both ancient and contemporary history tell the story. The Jewish people were thrown into the sea of the world's nations and until May 15, 1948, they had no country they could call their own. The descendants of Abraham have been persecuted as no other group of people in history. Many nations have tried to obliterate them as did Hitler, killing millions of Jews, and most recently, the Arab nations have engaged in war with Israel.

On more than one occasion, the Israeli people have been in a position where they could only say what Jonah said—"Out of the belly of hell cried I . . . for thou hast cast me into the deep in the midst of the sea; and the floods compassed me about: all thy billows and thy waves passed over me."

4. *Like Jonah, Israel has been wonderfully preserved.* Though every attempt has been made to swallow, assimilate and destroy the sons of Abraham, Isaac, and Jacob, yet, they are still with us. That their preservation has been miraculous goes without saying.

There is probably no city in the world that has suffered as much destruction as Jerusalem. "Since David's time, the city has been subject to forty-six sieges, seventeen of which have resulted in utter destruction and the leveling of Jerusalem to the ground."

Jesus predicted that Jerusalem would be trodden down of the Gentiles. Interestingly enough, the "Canaanitish name for Jerusalem was Jebus, which means a place trodden under foot." But Jesus put a time limit on His statement. He said, "until the times of the Gentiles be fulfilled." This capital city of Israel—this most prized and sacred city of the Jews—has been trodden down for centuries by the Gentiles.

And the whole story of Jerusalem is the story of the Israeli people as a whole—persecuted, buffeted, maligned, scattered, and many slain. But God has preserved the nation in spite of the fact that Israel's enemies had said, "Come, and let us cut them off from being a nation; that the name of Israel may be no more in remembrance" (Ps. 83:4).

The prophets had prophesied that Israel would not be completely destroyed. Jeremiah said, "For I am with thee, saith the Lord, to save thee: though I make a full end of all nations whither I have scattered thee, yet will I not make a full end of thee. . ." (Jer. 30:11). Again he said, "And I will gather the remnant of my flock out of all countries whither I have driven them, and will bring them again to their folds, and they shall be fruitful and increase" (Jer. 23:3).

The story of Israel is a story of preservation—

preservation in the belly of a great sea monster—preservation in the bowels of the Gentile world.

5. *Like Jonah, Israel's return to her assignment will be accompanied by great success.* In Romans 11:11-15, we read, "I say then, have they [Israel] stumbled that they should fall? God forbid: but rather through their fall salvation is come unto the Gentiles, for to provoke them to jealousy. Now if the fall of them be the riches of the world, and the diminishing of them the riches of the Gentiles; how much more their fullness? . . . For if the casting away of them be the reconciling of the world, what shall the receiving of them be, but life for the dead?"

No prophet so thoroughly predicts the restoration (resurrection) of the nation of Israel as Ezekiel. He uses the analogy of a great valley of dry bones. Those bones are made to live and to stand on their feet, "an exceeding great army." Then God says to Ezekiel, "These bones are the whole house of Israel: behold, they say, Our bones are dried, and our hope is lost." The prophecy continues, "Behold, O my people, I will open your graves, and cause you to come up out of your graves, and bring you into the land of Israel. . . . And shall put my spirit in you, and ye shall live, and I shall place you in your own land: then shall ye know that I the Lord have spoken it, and performed it, saith the Lord" (Ezek. 37:12-14).

That this prophecy concerning Israel is now

being fulfilled seems obvious. In the last twenty years her ruined places have been rebuilt, her waste places restored, her cities inhabited and her land cultivated. Palestine is blossoming as a rose and is becoming like the garden of Eden. All of this fits into the prophetic picture of Ezekiel, chapter 36.

But the restoration of Israel is not an end in itself. It is a means to an end—an end in which God will be glorified among all the nations of the world. It looks to that day when "the earth shall be filled with the knowledge of the glory of the Lord, as the waters cover the sea" (Hab. 2:14). It is a preface to that day in which, "many nations shall come and say, Come, and let us go up to the mountain of the Lord, and to the house of the God of Jacob; and he will teach us of his ways, and we will walk in his paths: for the law shall go forth of Zion, and the word of the Lord from Jerusalem. And he shall judge among many people, and rebuke strong nations afar off; and they shall beat their swords into plowshares, and their spears into pruninghooks: nation shall not lift up a sword against nation, neither shall they learn war any more. But they shall sit every man under his vine and under his fig tree; and none shall make them afraid: for the mouth of the Lord of hosts hath spoken it" (Mic. 4:2-4).

The work of the recommissioned Jonah led to the repentance of the great Gentile city of Nineveh. Even so, Israel's restoration to fellowship

with God and her new witness for God will lead
to a great work of God in the Gentile nations.

The experiences of Jonah are indeed prophetic and to those of us who live more than
twenty-five hundred years this side of Jonah, the
picture is clear. It would be difficult to conceive
of an object lesson of Israel's history more apt
than that of a swallowed (but unassimilated) and
regurgitated prophet. This is prophecy made
plain. The Book of Jonah is beyond question
right where it belongs—among the prophets.

LET'S DISCUSS

1. Why is the Book of Jonah included with the Minor
   Prophets?

2. Do you agree with the author's position that the Book
   of Jonah is a prophetic picture of events that would
   take place in Israel? Why, or why not? Give examples
   of how the history of Israel parallels the experiences
   of Jonah.

3. Ezekiel, chapters 36 and 37, contains many prophecies about the nation of Israel, some of which were
   fulfilled after the return from Babylonian captivity.
   Others seem to refer to the restoration of Israel as a
   nation. In your opinion, are these prophecies being
   fulfilled today? Explain your answer, giving specific
   examples.

4. Can you relate Romans 11:11-15 to the Book of
   Jonah? What parallels do you see between Jonah's
   experience and the passage in Romans?

3   About God

The name of God (in either the form Lord or God) appears thirty-nine times in the forty-eight verses of this book. Scattered evenly throughout the book, this would leave only nine verses in which the name would not be included. Furthermore, the book includes about twenty personal pronouns relative to God. We may, therefore, rightly assume that Jonah has much to say about God.

Though this is not a doctrinal book, it teaches us much doctrine. If we had no other access to Holy Writ—if the Book of Jonah were the only portion of Scripture available to us, we could still learn much about the character of God. Let us look at some of the more obvious lessons.

1. *Whoever else God is, He is one who communicates with man* and can be communicated with by man on a personal basis (1:1; 2:1).

This lies in direct accord with the rest of Scripture. The Bible is a "thus saith the Lord" book. It is filled with illustrations of God communicating with man and man communicating with God.

2. *The God of the Book of Jonah issues directives* which He expects to be obeyed (1:2).

This thought also harmonizes with the overall teaching of the Word of God. Delete the directives from Scripture and you have ruined the book.

3. *The God revealed in the Book of Jonah is knowledgeable of man's behavior* (1:2; 3:10).

Scripture is consistent in its teaching that nothing is hidden from God. Though sins are often committed behind closed doors or in some dark room, they are not unnoticed by God. All things are naked and open before Him.

4. *God reacts antagonistically to wickedness* (1:2).

God's condemnation of sin, and judgment upon the sinner, is a cardinal truth of Scripture. His attitude toward Nineveh as expressed in the Book of Jonah does not cause surprise in the mind of the student of Holy Writ.

5. *God's will can be resisted* (1:3, 10).

Jonah was neither the first nor the last "servant of God" to flee from the will of God. The Bible is replete with illustrations of varying degrees of disobedience on the part of the servants of the Lord. Saul and Samson are two of the more flagrant Old Testament illustrations of this fact.

6. *God has control over His creation and His creatures* (1:17; 2:10; 4:6-7, 10).

The fact that God is able to maneuver and manipulate the elements of nature as well as His creatures is everywhere recognized in the Word of God. God is never pictured as being indifferent to His creation. It is further noted that His manipulations (miracles) of nature are often related to His desire to accomplish some special purpose in the lives of those on whom He places special claim.

7. *He is the God of heaven and the creator of land and sea* (1:9).

This is a claim which the Bible maintains from Genesis to Revelation.

8. *God responds to man's judgment upon himself* (1:12-15).

Jonah suggested that the sea would cease its raging if the mariners would cast him overboard. This was Jonah's judgment upon himself. God responded to this judgment in the quelling of the storm and also in the preparing of the great fish to swallow Jonah. This coincides with Scripture which tells us that we should judge ourselves that we be not judged.

9. *God can be implored by the heathen* (1:14).

A vivid New Testament illustration of this truth is found in the story of Cornelius recorded in Acts 10. The angel of the Lord informed Cornelius that his alms and prayers had ascended unto God. God's response was to send Peter to Cornelius' household to enlighten him concerning the way of salvation.

10. *God does as He pleases* (1:14).

Scripture is steadfast in its affirmation that God does not have to give to man a reason for what He does. As the potter makes vessels to his own liking, so the Omnipotent One is free to do as He desires.

11. *God accepts worship, sacrifice, thanksgiving, and vows* (1:16; 2:9).

On no occasion does the Bible grant worship to men or angels. In those incidences in which attempts were made to worship men or angels, the attempts were immediately squelched.

12. *God can be prayed to from anywhere* (2:1).

Though the children of Israel were given a special place (the Tabernacle and later the Temple) in which to worship God, the Old Testament, as well as the New, provides numerous illustrations of men seeking the face of God in many places other than a temple or house of worship.

13. *God listens to the prayers of His people* (2:2).

"Thou heardest my voice," says Jonah. This suggestion of a prayer-hearing God is consistent with the teaching of Scripture concerning the nature of God. The psalms, the prophets and even the Old Testament historical books give repeated testimony to answered prayer. "Call upon me, and I will answer thee. . ." is a major chord in the harmony of Old Testament teaching.

14. *God punishes His servants who disobey Him* (2:3).

The truth that God chastises those He loves receives repeated emphasis in the Word of God.

15. *God must somewhere have a holy temple* (2:4, 7).

Jonah's statement, "Yet I will look again toward thy holy temple," immediately relates Jonah to his Hebrew background and to his knowledge of Israel's program of worship.

16. *God saves men from corruption and destruction* (2:6, 9).

Jonah's confession that "salvation [deliverance] is of the Lord," is equivalent to the testimony of Psalm 3:8, "Salvation belongeth unto the Lord." To this fact, Scripture gives repeated and irrevocable testimony.

17. *God sometimes gives His disobedient servants a second chance* (3:1).

This can be said of Israel as a nation as well as of numerous individuals whose biographies are recorded for us in the Word of God.

18. *God's message is one of judgment against sin* (3:2, 4).

From the account of the great flood until the final judgment day, the Bible is consistent in the presentation of the fact that God will not allow sin to go unjudged. The soul that sinneth shall die.

19. *God can be believed on by people whose previous knowledge of Him may have been very limited* (3:5).

There is no certain way for us to ascertain the amount of knowledge the Ninevites had about God. It is altogether possible that Jewish doctrine and teaching were known at least in part and at least by a few. It is hardly conceivable that the Assyrian Empire had not been influenced in part by the Jewish culture and religion. However, it was a very brief and limited message that caused the people to express their belief in God.

20. *God responds favorably to man's repentance* (3:10).

A clear call to repentance rings throughout the pages of the Bible. The sinful man has no access to God except via the path of repentance. In the Old Testament, repentance was accompanied by the shedding of the blood of animals. It is left to the New Testament to teach us that a Holy God can accept man's repentance only on the basis of the shed blood of the perfect Lamb of God.

21. *God can be described as being gracious, merciful, slow to anger, and of great kindness* (4:2).

This, of course, was not an original thought with Jonah. God had revealed Himself unto Moses on Mount Sinai as "The Lord, The Lord God, merciful and gracious, longsuffering, and abundant in goodness and truth, keeping mercy for thousands, forgiving iniquity and transgression and sin. . ." (Exod. 34:6-7). It is noteworthy that this revelation of God's nature was given on the very mount where His law was given.

22. *God is willing to reason with His wayward children* (4:4, 9-10).

The longsuffering of God in His dealings with Jonah exemplifies His longsuffering with the rest of His children. It reminds one of God's patience with the children of Israel in taking them through the wilderness.

23. *God is compassionate* (4:11).

It might be said with good reason that the basic message in the Book of Jonah is God's compassion for helpless, hopeless men and women. "Should I not spare Nineveh" is certainly an expression of the heart of God relative to His desire on behalf of all lost men everywhere and in every generation.

We would hardly expect a short, four-chapter history book to give us so much theology. But there it is—twenty-three interesting facts about God, all of which are consistent with the overall teaching of the Word of God. We are the richer because Jonah has been included in the canon of Scripture.

LET'S DISCUSS

1. Although the Book of Jonah was not written as a theological treatise on the character of God, God does appear as the preeminent person in the book. However, Jonah seems to steal the spotlight in the minds of most readers of the book. Do you agree? Why, or why not?

2. This chapter lists twenty-three things one can learn about God from the Book of Jonah. Which of these things seems most important to you? Give reasons for your answer.

3. Jonah 4:2 describes God as being gracious, merciful, slow to anger, and abundant in loving-kindness. Give illustrations from other Bible passages that also mention these qualities. Can you give other texts that illustrate the wrath and righteousness of God?

4. There are two occasions in the Book of Jonah in which God responded favorably to man's judgment upon himself (1:12-15; 3:10). What does this say to you about the character of God?

4 About Cities

Historians tell us that the Assyrian kingdom can be traced back to about 1400 B.C. This takes us back to the days of the Judges. However, Assyria was not a world power during the reigns of Saul, David, and Solomon over the united Kingdom of Israel. It was not until 900 B.C. under King Ashurnasirpal that it became a world empire. It then became the leading empire of the world for 300 years. This means that Assyria's rise to power began about the time of the divided kingdoms of Israel and Judah.

Shalmaneser was perhaps the first Assyrian king to come into direct and repeated conflict with Israel beginning about 860 B.C. Some of the later kings whose record of opposition to Israel is found in Scripture are Pul, Shalmaneser (the II), Sargon, Sennacherib, and Esar-haddon.

At the height of its power in the seventh century B.C., Assyria held sway over a vast territory of land covering Babylonia, Armenia, Syria, Cyprus, Arabia, Egypt, and parts of Media. That the kings of Israel and Judah were well known to the monarchs of the Assyrian Empire is attested to by Assyrian inscriptions which name

the following kings: Omri, Ahab, Jehu, Mena-
hem, Pekah, Hoshea, Ahaz, Hezekiah, and
Manasseh.

On four occasions, in the Book of Jonah, the
city of Nineveh is referred to as being "great." It
was great—great in its *prestige,* in its *prosperity,*
in its *power* and in its *perversion.*

1. *Prestige:* Nineveh was a city of great antiq-
uity. The Bible states that it was built by the
early descendants of Noah. "Out of that land
went forth Asshur, and builded Nineveh, and the
city Rehoboth, and Calah, and Resen between
Nineveh and Calah: the same is a great city"
(Gen. 10:11-12). This was hundreds of years
before the emergence of the Assyrian Empire.

Nineveh was probably built in the shape of a
parallelogram twenty to thirty miles in length
and ten to twelve miles in width. It lay on the
east bank of the Tigris River about two hundred
fifty miles north of the city of Babylon. Its
southern extremity stretched to the confluence
of the Tigris and the Upper Zab Rivers. This
included a number of villages and towns which
in twentieth-century terminology would be
thought of as suburbs.

The heart of the city proper covered an area
of only two and one-half miles by one and
one-half miles. This eight-mile circumference
was protected by five walls and three moats. The
inner wall was one hundred feet high (equal to a
modern ten-story building) and three chariots
could be driven side by side along the top of it.

Guesses as to the population of Nineveh have

varied greatly. The Jonah account simply says that there were more than "six score thousand [120,000] persons" who could not discern between their right hand and their left hand. Some theologians have taken this to refer to children and, hence, have estimated the population of the city to approximate six hundred thousand. Others have felt, however, that this would apply more accurately to the city proper and would not include the vast area of sixty miles in circumference in which the "suburbs" were found. They feel that the entire area probably encompassed a population close to the one million mark. Suffice it to say, Nineveh was a city of great prestige during the three hundred year period of the Assyrian Empire.

2. *Prosperity:* Nineveh's prosperity can hardly be overestimated. It was the commercial capital of the world. Its location on the Tigris River gave it access to the ocean and it lay in the path of the trade routes for the caravans of the East. Furthermore, it gained immense wealth from the Assyrian military conquests. It was common practice for conquering nations in those days to claim for themselves all the valuable possessions of a defeated people. Something more than a century after Jonah, Nineveh did this very thing to Israel's capital city of Samaria,[1] and to all the cities of Israel. The record of this is found in II Kings 18. Even King Hezekiah of Judah paid tribute to the Assyrian Empire. The prophet

---

[1] Northern Kingdom.

Nahum in chapters 2:9 and 3:19 speaks of the gold, the silver, the vast treasures, and the numerous merchants of Nineveh.

3. *Power:* For three centuries, Nineveh's military power was unmatched. The only armed forces that could give the Assyrians even token opposition were those of Egypt. And yet, of the Egyptians, Isaiah prophesied, "So shall the King of Assyria lead away the Egyptians prisoners and the Ethiopians captives, young and old, even naked and barefoot with their buttocks uncovered, the shame of Egypt" (Isa. 20:4).

Walls, towers, horses, chariots, shields, spears, and thousands of armed men suggest the military might of this great city.

In II Kings 19, we have the account of the destruction of just one of the great Assyrian armies. This army of 185,000 fighting men had besieged Jerusalem and had blasphemed God. The angel of the Lord then smote and destroyed the army (II Kings 19:35). Nor was this power unaccompanied by barbarous cruelty. According to one ancient authority, King Ashurnasirpal was reportedly accustomed to cutting off the hands, feet, noses, and ears of his captives. He then put out their eyes. He also seemed to delight in building mounds of human skulls.

4. *Perversion:* Nineveh was great in its perversion. It was filled with a perverse people whose whole way of life was perverted. Jonah 1:2 says, "their wickedness has come up before me." In *The Living Bible,* this has been paraphrased to

read "your wickedness rises before me; it smells to highest heaven."

This is similar to the description of Sodom and Gomorrah given in Genesis 18:20-21:

> "And the Lord said, Because the cry of Sodom and Gomorrah is great, and because their sin is very grievous; I will go down now, and see whether they have done altogether according to the cry of it, which is come unto me. . . ."

Sodom was given to all kinds of perversions and though God assured Abraham He would not destroy the city if but ten righteous people could be found in it, they were not found. And Nineveh was another Sodom.

The Bible has much to say about the depravity and perversity of human nature. Genesis 6:5, 11, and 12 picture it in these words:

> "And God saw that the wickedness of man was great in the earth, and that every imagination of the thoughts of his heart was only evil continually. The earth also was corrupt before God, and the earth was filled with violence. And God looked upon the earth and, behold, it was corrupt; for all flesh had corrupted his way upon the earth."

This is what God beheld as He looked upon the city of Nineveh.

Another classic description of human depravity is found in Romans 1:21-32:

> "Yes, they knew about him all right, but they wouldn't admit it or worship him or even thank him for all his daily care. And after awhile they

began to think up silly ideas of what God was like and what he wanted them to do. The result was that their foolish minds became dark and confused. Claiming themselves to be wise without God, they became utter fools instead. And then, instead of worshiping the glorious, ever-living God, they took wood and stone and made idols for themselves, carving them to look like mere birds and animals and snakes and puny men.

So God let them go ahead into every sort of sex sin, and do whatever they wanted to—yes, vile and sinful things with each other's bodies. Instead of believing what they knew was the truth about God, they deliberately chose to believe lies. So they prayed to the things God made, but wouldn't obey the blessed God who made these things.

That is why God let go of them and let them do all these evil things, so that even their women turned against God's natural plan for them and indulged in sex sin with each other. And the men, instead of having a normal sex relationship with women, burned with lust for each other, men doing shameful things with other men and, as a result, getting paid within their own souls with the penalty they so richly deserved.

So it was that when they gave God up and would not even acknowledge him, God gave them up to doing everything their evil minds could think of. Their lives became full of every kind of wickedness and sin, of greed and hate, envy, murder, fighting, lying, bitterness, and gossip. They were backbiters, haters of God, insolent, proud braggarts, always thinking of new ways of sinning and continually being disobedient to their parents. They tried to misunderstand, broke their promises, and were heartless—without pity. They were fully aware of God's death penalty for these crimes, yet they went right ahead and did them anyway, and

45

encouraged others to do them, too" (*The Living Bible*).

It seems evident that the people of Nineveh were aware of their evil ways. After Jonah's message reached the ears of the Assyrian king, he stepped down from his throne, put on sackcloth and ashes, and called upon everyone of his people to "turn from his evil ways, and from his violence and robbing" (Jonah 3:8).

But cities are more than prestige, prosperity, power, and perversion. Cities are people. People are savable. Therefore, cities are savable and the city of Nineveh demonstrates this. It gives lasting evidence that depraved and perverted men can repent. It suggests that your "Nineveh" and mine can be brought to God. It clearly demonstrates that God loves people and desires to deliver them and not to destroy them. "Christ," says Scripture, "came not to condemn the world but to save it." His message of deliverance must, therefore, be preached to all people by His people. The world's great sinful metropolises can and must be evangelized.

Yes, Jonah speaks about cities. He tells us in a vivid, unforgettable way that cities are people and that people need God. Furthermore, God needs people and He loves them enough to go after them.

LET'S DISCUSS

1. One writer described Nineveh in these words: "The passion to indulge was married to the passion to

46

acquire." Would you, using references from the Book of Nahum, agree with this description? Why would these passions be so offensive to the Lord? What can be done to combat the rising trend of satisfying personal appetites?

2. It seems that large cities often become spawning areas for all kinds of sin. What reasons would you give for this condition? How would you reverse that trend?

3. Would you say that the church today is meeting or neglecting its responsibility to big cities? Can a church minister effectively to both inner city people and to those living in suburbia? Give reasons for your answer.

4. What suggestions can you give for effective urban ministry?

5 About Human Nature

Jonah has some striking lessons to teach us about the religious intuitions and inclinations found in unregenerate human nature. The Assyrian kingdom was filled with sorcery, witchcraft, barbarous cruelty, idolatory, deceit, sensuality, and unmentionable moral perversions. The capital city of Nineveh was sold out to fleshly lusts and filthy lucre. The whole sordid picture does not vary a great deal from the view of human nature seen in every kingdom in every generation.

And yet with all the failures found in unregenerate man, there seems to be an accompanying desire for something better. This is seen in two episodes in the Book of Jonah.

First Episode

Witness the behavior of the sailors (mariners) as described in 1:4-16 (*The Living Bible*).

> But as the ship was sailing along, suddenly the Lord flung a terrific wind over the sea, causing a great storm that threatened to send them to the bottom. Fearing for their lives, the desperate sail-

ors shouted to their gods for help and threw the cargo overboard to lighten the ship. And all this time Jonah was sound asleep down in the hold.

So the captain went down after him. "What do you mean," he roared, "sleeping at a time like this? Get up and cry to your god, and see if he will have mercy on us and save us!"

Then the crew decided to draw straws to see which of them had offended the gods and caused this terrible storm; and Jonah drew the short one.

"What have you done," they asked, "to bring this awful storm upon us? Who are you? What is your work? What country are you from? What is your nationality?"

And he said, "I am a Jew; I worship Jehovah, the God of heaven, who made the earth and sea." Then he told them he was running away from the Lord.

The men were terribly frightened when they heard this. "Oh, why did you do it?" they shouted. "What should we do to you to stop the storm?" For it was getting worse and worse.

"Throw me out into the sea," he said, "and it will become calm again. For I know this terrible storm has come because of me."

They tried harder to row the boat ashore, but couldn't make it. The storm was too fierce to fight against. Then they shouted out a prayer to Jehovah, Jonah's God. "O Jehovah," they pleaded, "don't make us die for this man's sin, and don't hold us responsible for his death, for it is not our fault—you have sent this storm upon him for your own good reasons."

Then they picked up Jonah and threw him overboard into the raging sea—and the storm stopped!

The men stood there in awe before Jehovah, and sacrificed to him and vowed to serve him.

1. In the face of serious danger, the sailors cried unto their gods. They expressed a desperate hope that somehow, somewhere, there must be a being who could do something for them they could not do for themselves. Somewhere there must be a supreme being who is greater than the wind and the sea. It is altogether likely that these sailors lived carelessly, dishonestly, and perhaps even grievously sinful under ordinary conditions. Yet, they were prepared to call upon whatever gods they knew in their hour of helplessness.

In all of the great world religions (monotheistic, polytheistic, and pantheistic) there is abundant evidence that men possess the desire to identify with someone who is beyond them. The very existence of these religions testifies to this.

There are also numerous Biblical illustrations of this fact. Perhaps the most apt one is found in chapter 17 of Acts where Paul, after viewing the city of Athens, says, "Ye men of Athens, I perceive that in all things ye are too superstitious. For as I passed by, and beheld your devotions, I found an altar with this inscription, To the Unknown God. Whom therefore, ye ignorantly worship, him I declare unto you."

With all of the learning and enlightenment of the Greek nation and with all the philosophy the Epicureans and Stoics could share with the Greeks, there was still that within the hearts of the people that was not satisfied. An altar, therefore, was built to the unknown god in the hope that if they had neglected to worship some god, he would be appeased by this altar. Man seems to possess an innate desire to know God.

2. You will also note that when it came to a choice between the retaining of material possessions or life—possessions were discarded. The sailors were thus giving witness to the comparative value and sanctity of human life over things. Man seems to possess a deep desire to live at any cost. He has within him an intuitive sense of values which tells him that if he loses his life, he loses all. And yet, the paradox is that as long as he has life, he will spend it feverishly and sometimes foolishly in a mad and covetous passion for things. He, therefore, needs to be reminded that it profits a man nothing if he gains the whole world and loses his soul.

3. It is noteworthy that the sailors were not prepared to let Jonah sleep through this episode. Though they did not know that he was a Hebrew, yet they insisted that he must awake and call upon whatever god he might worship. This was a desperate expression of their hope that someone on board might have a god who would save them.

4. Verse 7 of this chapter presents a religious concept that is found in one form or another in almost all pagan religions. It is the concept that catastrophe is the judgment of the gods on man. This judgment is a result of the gods' displeasure with someone's misbehavior.

A further illustration of this concept is found

in Acts 28. The apostle Paul and his fellow shipmates had been wrecked on the island of Melita. While Paul was assisting others in the gathering of bundles of sticks, he was bitten by a deadly snake. "And when the barbarians saw the venomous beast hang on his hand, they said among themselves, No doubt this man is a murderer, whom, though he hath escaped the sea, yet vengeance suffereth not to live. And he shook off the beast into the fire, and felt no harm. Howbeit they looked when he should have swollen, or fallen down dead suddenly: but after they had looked a great while, and saw no harm come to him, they changed their minds, and said that he was a god" (Acts 28:4-6).

This cause and effect relationship between sin and judgment also includes the idea that many people may suffer because of the sin of one person. Jonah bears witness to the fact that this can be the case. Furthermore, the Bible consistently illustrates and exemplifies the truth that one person's evil or goodness does affect others. No man lives unto himself. Who he is and what he does inevitably relates to those he contacts. Nor can the gospel message itself be separated from this concept. All men are living either under the curse of the sin of the first Adam or within the salvation provided by the last Adam.

It must, however, be carefully noted that this "catastrophe-judgment" concept cannot always be applied. The religious witch doctors of all generations and of all religions have been notorious for their ability to pick out "scapegoats" or "Jonahs" upon whom they could lay blame for some local catastrophe—some earthquake, famine or plague—with the result that innocent victims often suffered.

It is sufficient, however, to know that in the account at hand, one man was responsible for the tragedy that overshadowed the others. Furthermore, he admitted it. "For my sake, this great tempest is upon you" (1:12).

The mariners were naturally determined to seek out the blameworthy person, whoever he was. And after all, if the gods were angry enough to pursue a guilty party, they must also be willing to reveal him. What better way could the revelation be made than by the casting of lots, or the drawing of straws.

Significantly enough, the casting of lots was not unknown in the Jewish religion. This is probably the way the sin of Achan was revealed (Josh. 7). An account of casting of lots is also given in I Samuel 14, where King Saul was seeking to discover the source of sin in the camp. Jonah, therefore, was not unaware of this method of doing things. Furthermore, a guilty conscience probably led him to react submissively to the fact that the lot fell upon him.

After the guilt had been established, the pagan mariners gave the guilty party an opportunity to explain himself. Furthermore, they invited him to pronounce his own condemnation. He fearlessly suggested that they should throw him into the raging sea. Then and then alone would the sea cease its raging. In spite of Jonah's confession and suggestion, the sailors rowed hard to get the ship to land.

Though this might suggest a quality of inherent kindness in the hearts of unregenerate men, it probably points more accurately to a basic religious fear. To comply with Jonah's request would be tantamount to sharing in an act of murder. And murder, even when the murdered party invites it, goes against the grain of even semienlightened moral standards. Furthermore, there was no way in which these men could be certain that Jonah's god would react favorably in response to throwing Jonah into the sea. The sailors, therefore, acted only when it became clearly evident that there was no other recourse.

It is then that the deepest religious trait in these men came to the surface. They prayed earnestly for deliverance from guilt before committing the act. They suggested to God that they were only doing that which He had made inevitable. Then the immediate miracle of a becalmed sea caused the men to fear the Lord exceedingly and they offered sacrifices and made vows unto Him.

While there is no Scriptural evidence that these pagan sailors ever became proselytes to Judaism or followers of the true God, it appears evident that unregenerate human nature is prepared to respond to the work and revelation of God under given circumstances. Unfortunately, those circumstances far too frequently seem to require signs and wonders and the Christian teaching is that true faith does not spring forth from, nor grow in, the soil of signs.

It can be only a matter of conjecture as to whether or not these awestruck Jehovah-fearing sailors went to Nineveh after this experience. Nor does it seem probable that they could have reached Nineveh via the sea routes more readily than Jonah. It is possible that the "living submarine" which the Lord prepared for Jonah, did a directed job of depositing its cargo comparatively close to Nineveh, either on the banks of the Tigris or on the West Coast of Palestine. However, if the sailors did reach Nineveh first, the story of their experience could account in part for Nineveh's almost immediate response to Jonah's message.

Second Episode

This brings us to chapter 3, from which we are able to make an additional observation as to the intuitive religious principles found in unregenerate human nature.

The reaction of Nineveh's king and people was one of repentance, a turning from evil, a self-humbling, fasting, sackcloth and ashes. They did this without any suggestion from God's messenger that they should do it. Furthermore, they did it without any promises that any good would accrue from it. This suggests an inward conviction which relates punishment with sin and forgiveness with repentance. Man seems to understand that God may act favorably toward those who depart from evil. It is, of course, difficult to determine with any great degree of certainty as to whether this understanding is born in human nature or whether it grows out of the influence of a culture which contains this concept.

Yes, Jonah has spoken—spoken about unregenerate human nature. And all he has told us is corroborated by the rest of Scripture. For this insight we are grateful.

LET'S DISCUSS

1. Do you think God hears the otherwise irreligious person who cries to God as a last resort in times of extreme and desperate need? Why, or why not?
2. Are all natural catastrophes due to sin? Can you point out specific instances from Bible history where God used a natural catastrophe as punishment? Are today's catastrophes, such as earthquakes, floods, typhoons, and hurricanes punishment sent by God? If so, is it ever possible to point to the reasons why God sent a natural disaster? Why, or why not?
3. Can a person who is running away from God still feel that God is taking care of him? Why was Jonah able to sleep soundly through a raging storm? What parallels can you find in a sleeping Jonah and sleepy Christians who hold the truth but do not speak it?
4. Is it possible to use the casting of the lot in a way that is pleasing to God? Does God direct the casting of lots in every situation?
5. Is Jonah's willingness to be thrown overboard tantamount to suicide? Do you think Jonah looked upon such action as a final escape from his predicament?

6 Of Religious Bigotry

Jonah was at one and the same time an Old Testament prodigal son and the prodigal's older brother. His prodigality was not that of overt acts of debauchery as seen in the New Testament prodigal. His prodigality was on a higher and more serious level. Jonah was no teen-age delinquent rebelling against the authority of an earthly father. He was a mature man of God to whom the will of God was plainly revealed. He acted in deliberate disobedience to the command of God. He disobeyed a divine directive and fled from God. He did this in the full knowledge that obedience to the directive could lead to the bringing of many people into fellowship with God. Surely there is no greater prodigality than that.

However, it is the prodigal's older brother to whom Jonah is most similar. The parable given by Jesus (Luke 15) tells us that when the older brother came to the house and heard the music and dancing, "he called one of the servants and asked what these things meant. And he said unto him, Thy brother is come; and thy father hath killed the fatted calf, because he hath received him safe and sound." The older brother's reaction was one of anger. When entreated by his father to rejoice with the others over the return of the prodigal, he answered, "These many years do I serve thee, neither transgressed I at any time thy commandment: and yet thou never gavest̄ me a kid, that I might make merry with my friends: but as soon as this thy son was come, which hath devoured thy living with harlots, thou hast killed for him the fatted calf."

And what a picture this is of Jonah's childish and bigoted refusal to respond to God's entreaty to him to rejoice in Nineveh's deliverance. There was no room for rejoicing in Jonah's heart over God's love for Nineveh. He felt he had every right to be angry even unto death over the issue of the Lord's compassion for that great city.

The story of the New Testament prodigal was not given for the sake of describing the distress or even the return of a wayward individual. It was given to lay bare the hypocrisy of Pharisaism as portrayed in the behavior of the older brother. Like the older brother, the Pharisees found room in their hearts only for wrath and condemnation against men and women who did not live according to the letter of the law, be they ever so repentant.

Pharisaism built a framework around the compassion of God and then said that if His love overflowed that framework, there was something wrong. The New Testament Pharisees believed there were certain days in which the compassion of God was not to be operative, i.e., the Sabbath. They also believed there were certain people unto whom the compassion of God was not to reach. Only those who were deserving of the love of God should experience it. And the Pharisees made up their minds as to who could or could not deserve that love.

Of course, this concept of the nature of God is absolutely contrary to the doctrine of both the Old and New Testaments. Yet it is seen in the lives of people in both books. It has also been prevalent in much of church history.

Though we have no Biblical record as to whether or not Jonah had children, yet the spiritual descendants of Jonah seem to appear on every hand. Strangely enough, they arise from the most unexpected circles. The following quote taken from the parable of the Good Samaritan (Luke 10) gives us a clear picture of two of Jonah's offsprings: "And by chance there came down a certain priest that way: and when he saw him, he passed by on the other side. And likewise a Levite, when he was at the place, came and looked on him, and passed by on the other side."

These self-righteous religious leaders both turned deaf ears and blind eyes to the suffering of a man who had been stripped, wounded, and left half-dead. It is not difficult to see the spirit of Jonah in that kind of behavior.

It is not, however, until we get close to the Lord's inner circle of Peter, James, and John that we see Jonah in boldest relief. The ninth chapter of the Gospel of Luke records the account of Christ's journey to Jerusalem. James and John were sent ahead into a small Samaritan village in order to prepare for the arrival of the Lord. But the Samaritans refused to accept James and John. This, the account tells us, was caused by the fact that Jesus was headed toward Jerusalem. The Samaritan refusal to accept Jesus into the village riled James and John. Their reaction is expressed in these words: "Lord, wilt thou that we command fire to come down from heaven, and consume them?" Jesus' answer to His disciples was, "Ye know not what manner of spirit ye are of." He followed this with a strong positive statement, "The Son of man is not come to destroy men's lives, but to save them."

Like Jonah, who was prepared to sit outside Nineveh and watch the Lord rain fire and brimstone upon the city, so James and John were prepared to see the judgment of God fall on a small Samaritan village. And all of this without any thought of the love of God and the compassion of the Savior toward lost men and women. It can be stated without fear of contradiction that if Jonah could have called down fire from heaven upon Nineveh, he certainly would have done it.

This same narrow, religious bigotry is seen in the life of Peter. Peter, who had been so close to his Lord; Peter, who had heard the Lord say, "For God so loved the world, that he gave his only begotten Son, that whosoever believeth in

him should not perish, but have everlasting life";
Peter, who had accepted Christ's command to go
into all the world and preach the gospel to every
creature; Peter, who had been baptized with the
Holy Spirit at Pentecost; Peter, who had not
only seen the Lord rise from the dead and ascend into heaven but who had also heard Him
say, "Ye shall be witnesses unto me both in
Jerusalem, Judea, Samaria, and unto the uttermost part of the earth"—this same Peter carried
within his heart much of the spirit of Jonah.
Perhaps it is not without significance that Peter's
name was, "Simon, son of Jonas."

Peter's provincial concept of the love of God
is demonstrated clearly in the tenth chapter of
Acts, where we are given the account of the
Lord endeavoring to send Peter to Caesarea in
order to lead Cornelius (a Gentile) to Christ. The
Lord gave Peter a vision of a great sheet let
down from heaven. This vision was repeated
three times. In each case, when Peter was told to
rise, kill, and eat the beasts thereon, his response
was, "Not so, Lord; for I have never eaten anything that is common or unclean." Peter's attitude toward the unclean food was also his
attitude toward the Gentiles. His reaction toward a commission to evangelize Cornelius
closely paralleled Jonah's attitude relative to
preaching in Nineveh.

It is probably safe to say that there were few
prophets in all Israel during Jonah's day who
would have acted any different than Jonah. And
it is likely that the majority of our Lord's dis-

ciples would have acted as Peter did had they been assigned to witness to Cornelius. The fact that Peter had to defend his actions before the apostles and believers at Jerusalem bears this out. Note Acts 11.

We refuse, however, to throw stones at Jonah or at the disciples of Christ. Beyond question, one of the great weaknesses in the church today is the presence of Jonah's spirit—that self-righteous spirit which puts doctrine and dogma ahead of compassion for the souls of men. Like the priest and the Levite in the parable of the Good Samaritan, we seem content to leave men and women by the roadside stripped, wounded, and half-dead, while we hurry hither and yon to preach about God's love. And all the time that message is limited to our own concept of what the love of God is. We seem quite willing to pull our own lambs out of the ditch on the Sabbath but like the Pharisees we react strongly if our Lord stoops to heal the withered hand of a needy individual. We too often manifest a self-righteous spirit which talks about identification with the cross, yet refuses to be identified with men and women who need the message of the cross.

It is altogether possible to become indignant at the sin of the world and yet do nothing to reach the sinner with the only message of deliverance that will help him. This is the spirit of Jonah. It is the spirit which led the Samaritan woman (John 4) to say, "The Jews have no dealings with the Samaritans." It is the spirit which causes the world today to feel that the church's message is no longer relevant.

The biggest trouble with Jonah was Jonah. He was his own greatest problem. The deceit in Jonah's heart was greater than the deceit in all of Nineveh. He was determined to preserve his own ideas of the love and righteousness of God even at the cost of running away from the will of God. He had made up his mind that the love of God should never be manifested toward the Assyrians. The Assyrians were enemies of the children of Israel and, hence, they were not to be loved; they were to be destroyed. There was no place for loving your enemies in Jonah's practice or preaching.

"The whole lesson of the book of Jonah is that of the sin of exclusiveness, the sin of imagining that if we have received light, it is for ourselves alone," says Dr. G. Campbell Morgan in his *Living Messages of the Books of the Bible* (Vol. I, Revell).

It was not that Jonah was ignorant of the greatness of God's love and compassion. He knew Israel's history well. He knew of the innumerable times the patience of God had been manifested toward the disobedient and stiff-necked people of Israel. He had accepted all of this for himself and for his people. But he would deny it to others. Jonah had created his own image of God. And though he knew better, he would hold to that image even at the cost of his life.

Jesus had no greater problem in His day than

the Pharisaism He found in Israel's religious circles. His strongest indictments were brought against the Pharisees. He told them the publicans and harlots would enter the kingdom of God before they. He accused them of shutting up the kingdom of heaven against men. He said that though they compassed sea and land to make one proselyte yet that proselyte became twofold more a child of hell than they. Jesus called the Pharisees blind guides of the blind. He accused them of cleansing the outside of the cup and platter but leaving the inside full of extortion and excess. He categorically stated that they were like whited sepulchres which appear beautiful on the outside but are full of dead men's bones and rottenness. He likened them unto a generation of serpents and vipers (Matt. 23).

From all of this it becomes plain that Pharisaism is deadly, dastardly, and dangerous. Nor are we without our share of it within the church today. We have yielded to the temptation of creating God in our image and of limiting infinite love to finite understanding. There is perhaps too much of Jonah's religious exclusivism in all of us.

Though the child of God must cling to truth tenaciously, he must be sure that it is truth and that it is not just his concept of truth. It must be truth in its infinite aspect. It must be truth unlimited by a religious bigotry or provincialism which places fences around the character of God.

Jonah was prepared to die for a principle. It was a religious principle based on his own finite concept of what God should do to Nineveh. Jonah would have saved himself a great deal of difficulty had he been ready to die for a person—the Person of God—instead of for a principle.

This is the only safe position for the Christian to take. Principles are significant in the Christian life insofar as they are related to the Person of Christ. Only those who can honestly say "For me to live is Christ," are in a position to die for the message they preach and for the Christ they love.

Like Paul before his conversion, we can sincerely and zealously give our lives to the promotion of a concept of God which proves to be wrong. But like Paul, we can also learn that to die for Christ is gain. There should be no room for bigotry in the lives of those who know that their salvation is all of grace and not of works and that the love of God is comprehensive enough to reach all men everywhere. We have no right to put a wall between the love of God and any man's soul whether that man is a friend or enemy. We must witness to our Nineveh regardless of the human excuses for not doing so.

LET'S DISCUSS

1. Jonah refused to go to Nineveh because he was afraid the people might repent. Did this reflect Jonah's nar-

rowmindedness, bigotry, prejudice, or desire to mold God after Jonah's likeness? Explain your answer.

2. Can you give examples of the Jonah spirit (putting doctrine and dogma ahead of compassion for men's souls) evident in the church today? How can this spirit be overcome?

3. Someone has said that Jonah typifies the expression: "If we cannot serve our way, we will not serve at all." Can you give other examples from Scripture of people who displayed this spirit? Is this attitude prevalent today? How may it be changed?

4. Is this evaluation fair: The biggest trouble with Jonah was Jonah. He was his own greatest enemy. To what extent would such a judgment be true of all of us?

7 About Prayer

There is much by way of explicit as well as implicit teaching on prayer in the Book of Jonah. The book contains three recorded prayers as well as a command to pray and a dialogue that might be considered prayer.

The first recorded prayer is that offered by the sailors before casting Jonah overboard—"Wherefore they cried unto the Lord, and said, We beseech thee, O Lord, let us not perish for this man's life, and lay not upon us innocent blood: for thou, O Lord, hast done as it pleased thee" (1:14).

It is noteworthy that these sailors who had so recently cried unto their gods now address Jonah's God. Circumstances had apparently led them to feel that Jonah's God is a prayer-hearing God. Furthermore, they plead their innocence before God in committing that which under other circumstances would be murder. They feel their action is forced upon them by a God who does as He pleases.

The sincerity in this prayer is seen in the fact that they made special effort ("rowed hard") to keep from having to throw Jonah overboard. It is also seen in their reaction after casting him into the sea—they "feared the Lord exceedingly, and offered a sacrifice unto the Lord, and made vows" (1:16).

There is a real sense in which the sailors' prayer was one of compulsion. It was forced upon them. They were driven to it by fear. They were not men who were versed in prayer. In all probability, they had never had access to the prayers of Abraham, Moses, or David. The straightforward earnestness of their prayer is therefore more significant than the theological content.

And yet there are lessons to learn from this brief prayer. We are told that the sailors "cried unto the Lord." There was intensity, heart, and emotion in their prayer. And these are some of the characteristics of true praying. Then, humility is suggested in the phrase "we beseech [beg] thee, O Lord." This is followed by a statement which indicates faith in the sovereignty of God—"thou, O Lord, hast done as it pleased thee." There is also a strong suggestion that the sailors recognized that there was a relationship of responsibility to God for taking a man's life. We should be grateful for the privilege of learning such lessons on prayer from men who would appear most incapable of teaching the subject to us.

We may assume that this simple prayer was answered not only because the "sea ceased from her raging," but also from the fact that there is no recorded judgment of God brought upon the sailors.

Before looking at the next recorded prayer as found in Jonah 2, we will do well to ask a few questions about prayer. These questions arise from the story given in chapter 1.

(1) Did Jonah pray before he bought his ticket to Tarshish?

(2) Did he pray before he lay down to sleep?

(3) Did he pray when the shipmaster commanded him to "Arise, call upon thy God"?

Though the probable answer is that he did not pray in any of these situations, yet is is possible that he prayed in all three of them. Prayer can become a meaningless routine and it is apt to become such when we are trying to cover our disobedience with a veneer of piety.

The second chapter of Jonah gives eight of its ten verses to Jonah's prayer. Even a hasty reading of the prayer reveals several noteworthy things. *First,* the brevity of the prayer. In light of the fact that Jonah was in the belly of the great fish for three days and three nights, this prayer which can be uttered in sixty seconds is surprisingly short. This would seem to strengthen the argument that Jonah did not live long in the fish.

Second, the prayer is characterized by agony, intensity, earnestness, and emotion. It is a prayer of desperation. Nor is it the only such prayer in the Bible. It reminds us of the prayer of Mordecai and Queen Esther when they heard of Haman's plot to destroy all the Jews. They resorted to three days and nights of fasting and agonizing prayer.

The desperation in Jonah's prayer also reminds us of some of David's prayers when he was being hounded by King Saul. Though David had been anointed to be the king of Israel, yet he was chased like a dog from cave to cave. Several of the psalms express the deep darkness of soul through which he passed and the earnestness with which he prayed.

The agony of Jonah's prayer also takes us to Gethsemane and Calvary where the Son of God poured out His soul as the billows and waves of God's wrath encompassed Him. "I am cast out of thy sight," cried Jonah. "My God, my God, why hast thou forsaken me?" cried Jesus.

Third, Jonah's prayer contains Scripture quotations. In Jonah's hour of deepest need, the psalms seemed to best express his heart cry.

Jonah said, "I cried by reason of my afflictions unto the Lord and he heard me." David said, "In my distress I cried unto the Lord and he heard me" (Ps. 120:1; note also Ps. 18:6).

Jonah said, "Out of the belly of hell [sheol, the place of the departed dead] cried I." David said, "The sorrows of death compassed me, and the floods of ungodly men made me afraid. The sorrows of hell [sheol] compassed me about. . ." (Ps. 18:4-5).

Jonah said, "All thy billows and thy waves

passed over me." David said, "All thy waves and thy billows are gone over me" (Ps. 42:7).

Jonah said, "I am cast out of thy sight." David said, "I am cut off from before thine eyes" (Ps. 31:22).

Jonah said, "The waters compassed me about, even to the soul: the depth closed me round about, the weeds were wrapped about my head." David said, ". . . the waters are come in unto my soul. I sink in deep mire, where there is no standing: I am come into deep waters where the floods overflow me" (Ps. 69:1-2).

Jonah said, " . . . yet hast thou brought up my life from corruption." David said, "For thou wilt not leave my soul in hell; neither wilt thou suffer thine Holy One to see corruption" (Ps. 16:10).

Jonah said, "Salvation is of the Lord." David said, "Salvation *belongeth* unto the Lord" (Ps. 3:8). In both of these cases, "Deliverance is Jehovah's" would more accurately express the thought.

Though the similarity of Jonah's prayer with those of David's argues that Jonah was a reader of the psalms, it also suggests the idea that the prayers of various people placed under similar pressures may very likely be expressed in similar language.

Fourth, Jonah's prayer is characterized by faith. In the midst of the unbearable, Jonah repeatedly expressed faith in the Lord his God. Note these statements:

1. "Out of the belly of hell cried I, and *thou heardest my voice.*"
2. "I said, I am cast out of thy sight; . . . *I will look again toward thy holy temple.*"
3. "I went to the bottoms of the mountains . . . *yet hast thou brought up my life from corruption.*"
4. "*I will sacrifice unto thee with the voice of thanksgiving: I will pay that that I have vowed.*"

A second look at Jonah's prayer convinces one that it is exactly the kind of a prayer that would grow out of the circumstances in which it was uttered. This was no Sunday morning benediction or Monday morning table grace. It was deadly earnest. It was brief, intense, Scripture-filled, and sprinkled with faith. Perhaps we need more of this brand of praying today.

As we turn now to Jonah 3, in search of further instruction on the subject of prayer, we come across one suggestive statement: "But let man and beast be covered with sackcloth, and cry mightily unto God: yea, let them turn every one from his evil way, and from the violence that is in their hands" (3:8).

This verse forms part of a royal edict given by a great pagan king who along with his people "believed God." That is, they believed the prediction delivered by Jonah that Nineveh would be overthrown in forty days. The people are commanded to "cry mightily unto God." And though we know they did, as verse 10 clearly implies, we are not given the content of their prayer.

The edict does, however, give us two definite implications concerning prayer which are consistent with the Biblical concept. First, the crying unto God was to be accompanied with fasting, sackcloth, and ashes. This suggests humility and penitence. Secondly, everyone was to turn from his evil ways. And this is an integral part of true repentance.

Though it can be said with certainty that the Assyrian king had never read II Chronicles 7:14, his behavior fell in direct line with the teaching of the verse. "If my people, which are called by my name, shall humble themselves, and pray, and seek my face, and turn from their wicked ways; then will I hear from heaven, and will forgive their sin, and will heal their land."

Jonah tells us that God responded to the faith and works (proof of repentance) of the Ninevites. In doing so, He remained true to His character. He did not *repent* of His plan to overthrow Nineveh for that plan was dependent upon Nineveh's wickedness. If the people of the city had remained in their wickedness, they would have been destroyed. By repenting, they put themselves in a position where God could refrain from destroying them and still remain true to His holy character.

Jeremiah 18:7-8 confirms this principle—"At what instant I speak concerning a nation, and concerning a kingdom, to pluck up, and to pull down, and to destroy it; If that nation, against whom I have pronounced, turn from their evil, I will repent of the evil that I thought to do unto them."

Note the similarity of Joel's appeal to Israel.

"Therefore also now, saith the Lord, turn ye even to me with all your heart, and with fasting, and with weeping, and with mourning: and rend your heart, and not your garments, and turn unto the Lord your God: for he is gracious and merciful, slow to anger, and of great kindness, and repenteth him of the evil. Who knoweth if he will return and repent, and leave a blessing behind him; even a meat offering and a drink offering unto the Lord your God?" (Joel 2:12-14).

This same principle is operable in God's dealings with individuals. We reap what we sow. If we sow to the flesh, we reap corruption. If we regard (hold) iniquity in our hearts, the Lord will not hear us. On the other hand, if we turn in repentance toward Him, we receive His favor. Prayer, then, is symbolized in uplifted, holy hands. And whether it is by an individual, a city, or a nation, God responds to that kind of praying.

The fourth chapter of this book gives us Jonah's second (and last) recorded prayer. It is a prayer that God would take his life—"Therefore now, O Lord, take, I beseech thee, my life from me; for it is better for me to die than to live." This desperate prayer grew out of the fact that Jonah's insatiable desire to see Nineveh destroyed was obviously being frustrated. He was not having his way in an issue concerning which he had deep convictions. And he would rather die than see his national loyalties and religious bigotries foiled.

One marvels that God does not answer such a prayer with swift judgment. On the other hand, such judgment would be a case of answering a fool according to his folly. Furthermore, it would be a contradiction of the graciousness and mercifulness of God. Jonah knew of God's mercy and it was for this reason that he had tried to run away from his God-given assignment. He says, "Therefore I fled before unto Tarshish; for I knew that thou art a gracious God, and merciful, slow to anger, and of great kindness and repentest thee of the evil" (4:2). Jonah had no doubt learned this truth from Exodus 34:6-7, where almost the same words are used to describe the character of God.

Though God and Jonah continue to carry on dialogue for the rest of chapter 4, it is debatable whether or not it could be called prayer. Nevertheless, it teaches us that God is reasonable with those with whom He communicates. In this whole conversation, Jonah is pouty but God is patient. Jonah is stubborn and selfish but God is long-suffering and gracious.

And who of us has not repeatedly acted like Jonah? Who of us has not tried the patience of God? Who of us has not ultimately rejoiced in the fact that His mercy endures forever?

The lessons on prayer gained from Jonah are many. But perhaps they can be summarized in this three-point outline. Prayer should be disciplined, delightful, and desperate.

1. Jonah would probably have avoided the hard experience which befell him had his decisions been directed by a disciplined prayer life. Acknowledging the sandtraps into which a rigid devotion to God can fall; admitting to the bondage of a legalistic prayer program, it still must be said that there is no substitute for a definite, determined, disciplined daily time with God. Anything less than this and prayer sluffs off into a careless "Good morning and good night" relationship with God.

It is inconceivable that Jonah could have spent an hour of true fellowship with God only to determine to disobey Him. His disobedience was not the root of broken fellowship with God—it was the fruit. Where there is no communion, there is confusion. Where there is no devotion, there is deviation. Where there is no fellowship, there is frustration. And it takes a glad but determined discipline to cultivate devotion.

2. Though Jonah says, "I will sacrifice unto thee with the voice of thanksgiving," yet there is very little delight in his prayer. And perhaps its absence is a lesson for us. Delight is that ingredient in devotion which makes communion with God meaningful. There is no higher exercise for the soul than to delight in the Lord and in His Word.

There is no substitute for rejoicing in the Lord—for singing unto the Lord—for giving thanks to the Lord. The desires of those who delight in the Lord will be fulfilled (Ps. 37:4). This is inevitable, for those who truly delight in the Lord will have desires that delight the Lord. Perhaps the psalms are best fit to assist us in this aspect of our devotion to God.

3. There are circumstances which call for desperation in the prayer life of the child of God. We have already alluded to this in our comments on Jonah's prayer.

In Jonah's case, his desperate prayer grew out of his desperate situation. This should not have to be the experience of the child of God. His desperation should grow out of his understanding of the desperate destiny of his fellow men. Their eternal condemnation should ring drops of agony out of his heart. Paul expressed this experience in these words, "I have great heaviness and continual sorrow in my heart. For I could wish that myself were accursed from Christ for my brethren, my kinsmen, according to the flesh" (Rom. 9:2-3).

Yes, discipline, delight, and desperation are essential to devotion. Two of these ingredients are missing in the prayers of Jonah. The tragic effects are evident. May they not be missing in our lives.

LET'S DISCUSS

1. In Jonah 1:14 we listen to a group of Gentile sailors pray to Jonah's God. How do you account for such a

prayer? Can you give Scriptural illustrations or references that indicate that God hears such prayers?

2. What outstanding characteristics can you find in Jonah's prayer (chapter 2)? Do you feel that people placed under similar pressures would be apt to express themselves in a similar way? Explain your answer.

3. Does the fact that Nineveh's people were instructed by their king to cry mightily unto God suggest an inherent (though perhaps limited) comprehension of a prayer-hearing, compassionate God? How do you explain such comprehension?

4. Jonah quoted a good deal of Scripture in his brief prayer. Discuss the pros and cons of quoting Scripture in both public and private prayers.

5. Does prayer change the will of God? What is the use of praying if God has all things planned?

6. How do you know when you are praying in the right way? How can you tell when you are asking for something simply to fill your own desires?

8 About Missions

The Book of Jonah dramatizes missions better than any other Old Testament book. It pinpoints the three basic elements of world evangelization. They are: (1) the character and corruption of men, (2) the character and compassion of God, and (3) the messenger and message of missions.

The condition of Nineveh as portrayed in the Book of Jonah is obviously analogous to the condition of the world. The Ninevites were a people without hope and without God. They were a materialistic people who lived without reference to things eternal. They were a perverted people whose lives were given to immorality and licentiousness. Their philosophy of life was "eat, drink and be merry, for tomorrow we die." Not that there were not some whose standards were higher than others. There doubtless were those in Nineveh whose consciences were sensitive to the law of God written therein. There possibly were some who were sincerely religious—men and women who offered their sacrifices and burned their incense to gods of wood and stone. There were others who made repeated efforts to live above the moral swamps in which most of their fellow men lived. But having said this, the very best that could be said of the populous of Nineveh was that it was godless—without God. And what a picture this is of all men of all generations who have not known the God of Abraham or Jesus Christ, His Son.

Our chapter on the subject of "Jonah Speaks about Cities" has dealt rather thoroughly with the subject of human depravity. We need not reiterate it. We need only to note that it is that very depravity which makes missions a necessity. World evangelization is not a program originated by man for his own benefit or well-being. On the contrary, it is a program originating in the heart of God in the light of man's total inability to lift himself out of his need. The basic message of missions is that man is a lost, condemned, and hell-bound sinner who is totally unable to provide a remedy for his condition.

Nineveh was a condemned city. The wrath and judgment of God was already determined upon it. This is the picture of all men everywhere—"condemned already."

But our story of missions as pictured in Jonah does not end with Nineveh's sad condition. We also have a revelation of the nature of God. And this is foundational to the missionary program.

God is first portrayed as a God of wrath. He is revealed as one who reacts antagonistically to sin. He is in revolt toward all unrighteousness.

He hates evil in every form and He is both able and determined to do something about it. He pronounces judgment against it.

God's judgment as pictured in the Book of Jonah was to be swift and complete. The stench of Nineveh's wickedness had reached the nostrils of God. That wickedness was not to be condoned. The soul that sinneth, it shall die and Nineveh was filled with men and women who were soon to receive the wages of their sin.

But the image of God as seen in the Book of Jonah is not limited to that of a righteous being who loves holiness and hates iniquity. We also see a glorious picture of the mercy of God. This is seen in God's willingness to warn the Ninevites of impending judgment. It is also revealed in His glad willingness to spare them when they turned to Him in repentance. The story unveils the God who is merciful, gracious, slow to anger, and of great kindness.

Where would missions be without this kind of a message? The love and mercy of God are absolute essentials to the missionary message. Apart from them, there would be no world evangelism. They represent as nothing else the unique aspect of the Christian gospel. It is in them the Good News is found. If there is one thing above all others that the Book of Jonah has to tell us it is that God is a God of compassion—that the height and depth, length and breadth of the love of God cannot be measured—that His mercy endureth forever, and that He approaches all men with outstretched arms.

"Come let us reason together, saith the Lord. Though your sins be as scarlet, they shall be white as snow; though they be red like crimson, they shall be as wool" (Isa. 1:18). "Look unto me, and be ye saved, all the ends of the earth: for I am God, and there is none else" (Isa. 45:22). "Come unto me, all ye that labour and are heavy laden, and I will give you rest" (Matt. 11:28). These are but a few expressions of God's invitations to all men. This message of the love of God is basic to the program of missions and is exemplified in God's compassion for repentant Nineveh.

God was both the author and the producer of Jonah's dramatic story. Paramount to all other reasons for which this historical event was brought to pass is that of vividly portraying the compassion of God for lost men. And, "Should not I spare Nineveh" is the verbal expression of that compassion.

If Almighty God has one supreme desire, it is to bring lost men and women within the fold of His love. Calvary's cross is the cardinal proof of this. "God commendeth his love toward us, in that, while we were yet sinners, Christ died for us" (Rom. 5:8).

But the need of men and the love of God must be brought together. How can men call on Him of whom they have not believed and how can they believe on Him of whom they have not heard? There must be a go-between—an ambassador. Jonah was appointed to be the ambassador to Nineveh. But Jonah had reasons—strong reasons—why he did not want to fulfill his God-given assignment. At least three reasons suggest themselves.

1. A theological provincialism which insisted that Israel alone should be a recipient of the mercy of God. As we have already pointed out, this provincialism seemed to be deeply ingrained in the minds of Israel's people. It was an exclusivism which fenced in the love of God.

2. Jonah possessed a deep-seated hatred of the Assyrians. Previous to and during all of Jonah's life, Assyria was the ruling empire of the world. The Assyrians wielded a cruel and devastating authority in every nation they overran. Jonah not only knew what the Assyrian kings had done in the past but he also had strong convictions as to what they would do in the future. There was no doubt in Jonah's mind that Assyria was a deadly enemy. Nothing therefore could have been more satisfactory to him than to have the Assyrian capital city of Nineveh destroyed.

3. Jonah doubtless held within his heart a fear that his ministry to Nineveh might fail. Before his attempted flight from his assigned task, he had argued with God (4:2) about this very fact. Jonah knew altogether too well that God was merciful and longsuffering and that if the people of Nineveh repented, He would withhold judgment from them. This would appear to make Jonah's prophetic ministry a failure. If

Nineveh was not destroyed, then Jonah's reputation as a prophet would be affected. It is altogether possible that Jonah had more respect and concern for his own reputation than he did for the glory of God or salvation of Nineveh.

Certainly one thing is clear in this study of Jonah and that is that God's greatest obstacle to the conversion of Nineveh was not to be found in Nineveh. It was not to be found in the jails, the gambling dens, the saloons, or even the houses of ill-fame in that city. God's greatest obstacle in turning Nineveh to repentance was not found in the graft-ridden police force, the corrupt politics, the juvenile delinquency, or even the idolatrous temples of the city. God's biggest obstacle was found in the pious, prejudiced heart of Jonah.

It is not always sin in the hearts of sinners that keeps men from turning to God. It is sometimes sin in the hearts of saints. It is impossible to estimate how much the fulfilling of the great commission has been hindered by the disobedience of the children of the Lord.

It goes without saying that a self-centered Christianity is Satan's pattern, not God's. God scattered the early church by means of persecution in order to protect her from the danger of being wrapped up in herself. With a world that desperately needs the gospel message, we need ever to be alert to the danger of establishing our little Protestant monastaries and building walls around our message.

Yes, Jonah speaks of missions. He tells us that a loving and righteous God has commissioned us to preach to a needy and unrighteous world. He tells us that disobedience to that commission will not go unpunished. He tells us that God will show mercy upon whom He will show mercy whether it fits our prejudices or not. He tells us that God is depending on us to deliver the message.

LET'S DISCUSS

1. What is there about the character of God that makes the program of world evangelism mandatory? What characteristics of human nature also suggest the importance of world evangelism?

2. The people of Nineveh were given an opportunity to repent. It seems that the people of Sodom and Gomorrah were not given that opportunity (Gen. 19). Would you say that this is evidence of inconsistent treatment for the same sins? Give reasons for your answer.

3. How does one reconcile God's wrath toward sin and His mercy toward sinners? What other Biblical illustrations can you suggest which reveal both the wrath and the mercy of God?

4. What do Jonah's reasons for not wanting to go to Nineveh say to the church today about theological provincialism, religious and racial prejudices?

5. It seems that Jonah was God's greatest obstacle to the reaching of Nineveh. In what ways are believers today obstacles to the fulfilling of the Great Commission?

9   Of Spiritual Values

It is not without significance that the key word in Jonah's flight from God is *down*. He went *down* to Joppa. He went *down* onto the ship. And he went *down* into the hold thereof. It is hardly conceivable that a flight from the High and Holy One could be in any other direction than down. In what direction is your spiritual condition moving?

Jonah 1:3, "... he found a ship going to Tarshish." All the time Jonah was hurrying to Joppa he was rationalizing his flight from God. Before he ever reached Joppa's harbor he had made up his mind that if he found a ship ready to sail to Tarshish then somehow his actions must be fitting into the will of God. Like a lot more of us, he had not learned that the ready way is not always the right way. We have an enemy who is delighted to make our backsliding convenient.

Jonah 1:3, "... so he paid the fare thereof. . . ." Though Jonah gave the ship's purser the full amount for his ticket to Tarshish, he failed to take account of the price he would have to pay for running from the will of God. Jonah paid for his disobedience for the rest of his life. One of the payments was to write the confession of his failure in bold letters for all to read. It costs to obey God—it costs more to disobey Him. Think twice about the price of disobedience. You may have to pay for it for a long while to come.

Jonah 1:3, ". . . to go with them . . . from the presence of the Lord."

1. Jonah was in the *wrong conveyance.* He should have been on a ship of the desert (camel) instead of in a ship on the sea.

2. He was keeping the *wrong company.* At a time when he needed the fellowship of believers he was surrounded with idolaters.

3. Jonah was going to the *wrong city.* Not that Tarshish didn't need God but that God's assignment for Jonah at that time was Nineveh.

God told Jonah to go east but he went west.

God told him to go to a city but he went to sea.

God told him to stand up and preach but he lay down and slept.

How disobedient can we get?

Jonah 1:4, ". . . the Lord sent out a great wind . . . a mighty tempest in the sea, so that the ship was like to be broken."

Not all the storms of life are God-sent. Paul experienced a severe storm and shipwreck on his way to Rome. Obviously, it was an effort of Satan to keep Paul from reaching his destination. But God overruled. However, much of our suffering is self-afflicted. Like Jonah, we have disobeyed or headed in the wrong direction and God has had to bring chastisement into our lives to get us back on the right track.

The Bible pictures for us—

1. Jonah in a storm—asleep.
2. The disciples in a storm—afraid.
3. Paul in a storm—a witness.

Where do you fit into this picture?

Jonah 1:5, ". . . he lay, and was fast asleep."

Be careful of where and how you sleep. Samson slept with his head on Delilah's lap and lost his power with God and man. The disciples slept in the Garden of Gethsemane when they should have been watching and praying. Then they fled in the hour of their Master's greatest need.

More than one servant of God has failed in Christian service because of undisciplined sleep. He had slept too little and become overly tired or he had slept too much and neglected his time alone with God.

Jonah 1:6, "What meanest thou, O sleeper? arise, call upon thy God. . . ."

There is something ironical about the fact that the man who was the cause of the storm could sleep through it. And there is something alarming about the fact that the godless (the mariner) had to call on the godly (Jonah) to pray. But perhaps this is more often the case than we realize. Paul wrote to the Corinthian Christians, "Awake to righteousness, and sin not; for some have not the knowledge of God: I speak this to your shame" (I Cor. 15:34). How applicable is this to your church and mine today?

Jonah 1:8, "What is thine occupation? . . . whence comest thou? . . . what is thy country? and of what people art thou?"

Jonah apparently felt the first three questions were irrelevant so he went immediately to the fourth. He answered, "I am an Hebrew; and I fear the Lord, the God of heaven, which hath made the sea and the dry land."

It is important to be able to discern the irrelevant and to get to the point with a clear-cut testimony. However, it is a tragedy when a statement of faith has to be coerced from us as a result of our misbehavior. In saying, "I am an Hebrew," or "I am a Christian," we are admitting to a standard of behavior that should influence our walk and glorify God.

Jonah 1:10, "Why hast thou done this?"

The law of cause and effect is one of God's immutables. Whatever a man sows, that he also reaps. Sad it is when the tares we sow grow in another man's field. But seldom are others not affected by the evil we do, for no man lives unto himself.

There is real pathos in the question, "Why did you do it?" And that pathos is deepened when the question comes from an unbeliever. Perhaps a bit of personal reflection on the motives back of our behavior would save us from misbehavior. The answer to "Why do I want to do this?"

could keep us from having to answer for that about which we would be ashamed. As has been aptly said, "An ounce of prevention is worth a pound of cure."

Jonah 1:12, ". . . for my sake this great tempest is upon you."

There is no substitute for a straightforward confession. "He who hides his sin," says the Bible, "shall not prosper." Hidden or unconfessed sin inevitably leads to more sin. Our sin may be buried, as Achan's was (Josh. 7), in the floor of our tent or in the depth of our hearts, as Ananias and Sapphira's was (Acts 5), but it is never hidden from Him who sees all things.

The only way to really hide sin is to confess it and let God bury it in the depths of the sea. "If we confess our sins, he is faithful and just to forgive us. . ." (I John 1:9). It is not easy to say, "I am to blame," or "I have sinned," but it is the only path to forgiveness and peace.

Jonah 1:14, "for thou, O Lord, hast done as it pleased thee."

Many frustrations of life disappear when a person gladly places his faith in the sovereignty of God. The Christian who argues against God's right to do as He pleases argues against the plain teaching of the Bible. Furthermore, he will probably find many of his own experiences as a child of God difficult to explain apart from God's sovereignty.

This does not suggest that God is capricious. His actions all stem from absolute omniscience and infinite love. When He does as He pleases it is always for our eternal good and for His great glory. As has been suggested, He is too wise to make mistakes and too loving to be unkind.

Jonah 2:1, "Then Jonah prayed. . . ."

This prayer was not offered in the temple or in a synagogue. It was not prayed on a mountain top or on a street corner. Nor was it the kind of prayer that would have been prayed at any of those places. This was a prayer of desperation prayed without the benefit of a kneeling pad, pew, or altar.

And how very unnecessary this very necessary prayer was. Had Jonah prayed as earnestly before he started on his flight from God, he never would have fled and the necessity for such a prayer never would have arisen. Sad it is that our most earnest prayers grow out of our most difficult circumstances—circumstances that would not have occurred had earnest prayer preceded them. Prayer can keep us from those "then Jonah prayed" situations.

Jonah 2:2, ". . . I cried by reason of mine affliction . . . and He heard me."

It is true that suffering serves the soul. Affliction is a rod in the hands of the heavenly Father with which He chastises His children. It is just as wrong for Him to "spare the rod" and "spoil the child" as it is for an earthly parent. Whom He loves He chastises.

It was affliction that repeatedly brought Israel back to God. When they cried unto Him in their affliction He saved them out of their trouble. (Note the Book of Judges.) God afflicts us in order to instruct us.

Jonah 2:4, "... I am cast out of thy sight...."

There certainly can be no deeper cause for despair than that which stems from a feeling of being cast out of God's sight. The deepest suffering and the darkest hour of our Lord's days on earth are revealed in the words, "My God, my God, why hast thou forsaken me." In this case, it was our sins which separated the Savior from His Holy Father.

Though sin can break our fellowship with God—though it can shorten His arm and deafen His ear, there is no reason for us to continue in broken fellowship. Confessed sin restores communion. And He has promised never to leave us or forsake us. We must not trust our feelings when they contradict His promise, "Lo, I am with you alway."

Jonah 2:8, "They that observe lying vanities forsake their own mercy."

Wise is the man who learns early and well that all decisions made outside of the will of God are detrimental to his own life. There is no surer way for a man to forsake his own welfare than to turn from the truth of God. Romans gives us a picture of what happens to men when they reject the knowledge of God and turn to their own ways.

The lives of Samson, Saul, Jonah, and others illustrate the tragedy that pursues those who observe lying vanities, and the worship of, or obedience to, anything other than God is a lying vanity.

Jonah 2:9, "But I will sacrifice unto thee with the voice of thanksgiving."

It is impossible to exaggerate the importance of thanksgiving in our relationship to God. The psalmist said, "It is a good thing to give thanks unto the Lord." Paul said, "In everything, by prayer and supplication with thanksgiving let your requests be made known unto God."

But thanksgiving becomes a sacrificial offering when, like Jonah's, our circumstances preclude any apparent reason for thanksgiving. Daniel illustrates this vividly. When the word reached him that all who made any request from anyone other than King Darius would be thrown to the lions, he went to his room, fell upon his knees and "gave thanks before his God, as he did aforetime" (Dan. 6:10). Daniel knew that such an act would send him to the lions' den but he did it.

Paul and Silas offered the sacrifice of thanksgiving to God as they sang His praises in the jail at Philippi (Acts 16). Thanksgiving is most meaningful when it costs the most.

Jonah 2:9, "Salvation is of [Jehovah] the Lord."

What Jonah has really said is, "Salvation is of the Savior." And no one could have spoken with more authority from the physical point of view. If Jonah was to be delivered (saved) from the belly of the great fish, his deliverance must come from God alone. There was nothing—absolutely nothing—Jonah could do to deliver himself.

And this is analagous of salvation from the spiritual angle. There is nothing man can do to wash away the guilt of his sin or to deliver himself from its bondage and ultimate damnation. He is helpless and without hope. Salvation comes from God alone. This is the unique message of Christianity.

Jonah 3:2, ". . . preach unto it the preaching that I bid thee."

The messenger of God has no more sacred responsibility than that of making sure his message is from the Lord. It is his duty to be able to say with Paul, "that which I have received of the Lord, the same declare I unto you."

It was Paul who also said, "I am determined to know nothing among you save Jesus Christ and him crucified." This is the heart of the preacher's message. To alter that message, or to substitute something else for it, is to become a false prophet. And, "if any man preach any other gospel, let him be accursed."

Where are those servants of the Lord today whose holy zeal compels them to echo the words of the apostles, "We cannot but speak the things which we have seen and heard" (Acts 4:20). Or where are those preachers whose intimacy with God enables them to say to their congregations, "that which we have seen and heard declare we unto you" (I John 1:3).

Jonah 3:4, "So the people of Nineveh believed God. . . ."

94

Many years after Nineveh's repentance, Jesus said, "the men of Nineveh shall rise in judgment with this generation, and shall condemn it: because they repented at the preaching of Jonas; and, behold a greater than Jonas is here" (Matt. 12:41).

There is no doubt that Nineveh's repentance is one of the most remarkable accounts in religious history of a pagan people turning to God. And it took place under the preaching of a disobedient prophet. How much more our Lord's generation should have repented under His preaching. How much more serious will their condemnation be in light of the Light they rejected. And what about our generation with all the truth to which it has been exposed.

Belief in God unaccompanied by repentance is no belief at all.

Jonah 3:5, ". . . and put on sackcloth, from the greatest of them even to the least of them."

Genuine religious awakenings have a way of leveling people. True conversion makes brothers out of bankers and ditch diggers; out of the educated and the illiterate.

Revival within the church brings people together in a spirit of oneness. Differences are forgotten when Christ becomes supreme in a group of believers.

Jonah 3:10, ". . . and God repented of the evil, that he had said he would do unto them; and he did it not."

God's change of attitude came as a result of Nineveh's change of action. The people of Nineveh turned from their evil ways and looked toward God in repentance. God's response was in keeping with His character. Jeremiah 18:7-8 gives us the picture. "At what instant I shall speak concerning a nation, and concerning a kingdom, to pluck up, and to pull down, and to destroy it; if that nation, against whom I have pronounced, turn from their evil, I will repent of the evil that I thought to do unto them."

Jonah 4:1, "But it displeased Jonah exceedingly, and he was very angry."

Jonah's anger and displeasure grew out of God's goodness to Nineveh. It is an alarming fact that one who is a recipient of so much of the love of God can begrudge it to others. And yet this is happening every day of every Christian's life. Our withholding of, and refusal to share, the message of God's grace to nations and peoples who so desperately need it is a proof of this. We are as guilty as Jonah in our unwillingness to love our enemies. And who of us really cares when tragedy strikes an enemy nation? There is far more of Jonah in all of us than we are ready to admit.

Jonah 4:3, ". . . for it is better for me to die than to live."

A choice of death over life may stem from many sources. Here are a few of them:

1. A deep sense of social ostracism.
2. An incurable disease.
3. Unendurable pain.
4. Fear of an enemy.

5. Realization of serious failure.
6. Pressure and nervous tension.
7. Spite, envy, or jealousy.
8. An inordinate desire for pity.
9. Discouragement and hopelessness.
10. A broken heart over some great disappointment or loss.

But there should not be room for any of these things in any abiding way in the life of the Christian. "To live is Christ," should provide the motivation of his life.

Jonah 4:6-8

"And the Lord God prepared a gourd. . . ."

"But God prepared a worm. . . ."

"God prepared a vehement east wind. . . ."

A pouting child is never helped by pampering.

The gourd (vine) changed Jonah's grief to gladness. The worm and the east wind cast him into despair.

It is doubtful that Jonah was aware that the changing circumstances which crossed his path were God-prepared. It might have affected his whole reaction had he realized that the Lord was trying to communicate with him by means of the experiences through which he was passing.

Happy is the man who can face the pleasant and the unpleasant with an unwavering confidence in God. Blessed is the man who really believes that all things work together for good to those who love Him. Wise is the man who places every circumstance within the circumference of God's goodness and omniscience.

Jonah 4:11, " ... should not I spare Nineveh. . . ?"

This question is the Old Testament way of saying, "For God so loved the world. . . ." Or perhaps better yet, it is the Old Testament way of saying, "But God commendeth his love toward us, in that, while we were yet sinners, Christ died for us."

The Bible's message from beginning to end is one of God's love for sinful men. He indeed hates sin but loves the sinner. He has done everything omnipotence can do to make the sinner's salvation possible.

God is love and when He loves it is but the natural expression of His supernatural being. The height, depth, length, and breadth of His love cannot be computed but it can be experienced. We can experience His love for us and His love for others can be manifest through us.

The next time you look at the Nineveh in which you live with discouragement, contempt, or even hate, remember God's compassion for the lost souls therein. Give Him the right to love them through you.

LET'S DISCUSS

1. Do you agree with this assertion: "It costs to obey God—it costs more to disobey Him." Give reasons why you answer as you do.

2. What happens to the person who tries to run away from God, or from the path of duty?

3. The story of Jonah is an excellent illustration of the saying, "No man is an island." What implications should this truth have for your life?

4. Does God communicate to us through some of the experiences that come our way? Explain your answer. What judgments has the Lord brought upon the world in modern times?

5. What is the most significant lesson you have learned from your study of the Book of Jonah?

JONAH SPEAKS—

The following text of the Book of Jonah taken from *The Living Bible** is printed with wide margins to encourage you in your study of the book. A careful study of this paraphrase of Jonah is destined to bring rich blessing to you.

1 *The Lord sent this message to Jonah, the son of Amittai:*

² "Go to the great city of Nineveh, and give them this announcement from the Lord: 'I am going to destroy you, for your wickedness rises before me; it smells to highest heaven.' "

³ But Jonah was afraid to go and ran away from the Lord. He went down to the seacoast, to the port of Joppa, where he found a ship leaving for Tarshish. He bought a ticket, went on board, and climbed down into the dark hold of the ship to hide there from the Lord.

⁴ But as the ship was sailing along, suddenly the Lord flung a terrific wind over the sea, causing a great storm that threatened to send them to the bottom. ⁵ Fearing for their lives, the desperate sailors shouted to their gods for help and threw the cargo

*Used by permission of Tyndale House, Publishers Wheaton, Illinois.

overboard to lighten the ship. And all this time Jonah was sound asleep down in the hold.

⁶ So the captain went down after him. "What do you mean," he roared, "sleeping at a time like this? Get up and cry to your god, and see if he will have mercy on us and save us!"

⁷ Then the crew decided to draw straws to see which of them had offended the gods and caused this terrible storm; and Jonah drew the short one.

⁸ "What have you done," they asked, "to bring this awful storm upon us? Who are you? What is your work? What country are you from? What is your nationality?"

⁹,¹⁰ And he said, "I am a Jew; I worship Jehovah, the God of heaven, who made the earth and sea." Then he told them he was running away from the Lord.

The men were terribly frightened when they heard this. "Oh, why did you do it?" they shouted. ¹¹ "What should we do to you to stop the storm?" For it was getting worse and worse.

¹² "Throw me out into the sea," he said, "and it will become calm again. For I know this terrible storm has come because of me."

¹³ They tried harder to row the boat ashore, but couldn't make it. The storm was too fierce to fight against. ¹⁴ Then they shouted out a prayer to Jehovah, Jonah's God. "O Jehovah," they pleaded, "don't make us die for this man's sin, and don't hold us responsible for his death, for it is not our fault—you have sent this storm upon him for your own good reasons."

¹⁵ Then they picked up Jonah and threw him overboard into the raging sea—and the storm stopped!

¹⁶ The men stood there in awe before

Jehovah, and sacrificed to him and vowed to serve him.

¹⁷ Now the Lord had arranged for a great fish to swallow Jonah. And Jonah was inside the fish three days and three nights.

2 THEN JONAH PRAYED to the Lord his God from inside the fish:

² "In my great trouble I cried to the Lord and he answered me; from the depths of death I called, and Lord, you heard me! ³ You threw me into the ocean depths; I sank down into the floods of waters and was covered by your wild and stormy waves. ⁴ Then I said, 'O Lord, you have rejected me and cast me away. How shall I ever again see your holy Temple?'

⁵ "I sank beneath the waves, and death was very near. The waters closed above me; the seaweed wrapped itself around my head. ⁶ I went down to the bottoms of the mountains that rise from off the ocean floor. I was locked out of life and imprisoned in the land of death. But, O Lord my God, you have snatched me from the yawning jaws of death!

⁷ "When I had lost all hope, I turned my thoughts once more to the Lord. And my earnest prayer went to you in your holy Temple. ⁸ (Those who worship false gods have turned their backs on all the mercies waiting for them from the Lord!)

⁹ "I will never worship anyone but you! For how can I thank you enough for all you have done? I will surely fulfill my promises. For my deliverance comes from the Lord alone."

¹⁰ And the Lord ordered the fish to spit up Jonah on the beach, and it did.

3 THEN THE LORD spoke to Jonah again: "Go to that great city, Nineveh," he

said, "and warn them of their doom, as I told you to before!"

³ So Jonah obeyed, and went to Nineveh. Now Nineveh was a very large city, with extensive suburbs—so large that it would take three days to walk around it.

⁴,⁵ But the very first day when Jonah entered the city and began to preach, the people repented. Jonah shouted to the crowds that gathered around him, "Forty days from now Nineveh will be destroyed!" And they believed him and declared a fast; from the king on down, everyone put on sackcloth—the rough, coarse garments worn at times of mourning.

⁶ For when the king of Nineveh heard what Jonah was saying, he stepped down from his throne and laid aside his royal robes and put on sackcloth and sat in ashes. ⁷ And the king and his nobles sent this message throughout the city: "Let no one, not even the animals, eat anything at all, nor even drink any water. ⁸ Everyone must wear sackcloth and cry mightily to God, and let everyone turn from his evil ways, from his violence and robbing. ⁹ Who can tell? Perhaps even yet God will decide to let us live, and will hold back his fierce anger from destroying us."

¹⁰ And when God saw that they had put a stop to their evil ways, he abandoned his plan to destroy them, and didn't carry it through.

4 THIS CHANGE OF plans made Jonah very angry. ² He complained to the Lord about it: "This is exactly what I thought you'd do, Lord, when I was there in my own country and you first told me to come here. That's why I ran away to Tarshish. For I knew you were a gracious God, merciful,

slow to get angry, and full of kindness; I knew how easily you could cancel your plans for destroying these people.

³ "Please kill me, Lord; I'd rather be dead than alive [when nothing that I told them happens]."

⁴ Then the Lord said, "Is it right to be *angry* about *this?*"

⁵ So Jonah went out and sat sulking on the east side of the city, and he made a leafy shelter to shade him as he waited there to see if anything would happen to the city. ⁶ And when the leaves of the shelter withered in the heat, the Lord arranged for a vine to grow up quickly and spread its broad leaves over Jonah's head to shade him. This made him comfortable and very grateful.

⁷ But God also prepared a worm! The next morning the worm ate through the stem of the plant, so that it withered away and died.

⁸ Then, when the sun was hot, God ordered a scorching east wind to blow on Jonah, and the sun beat down upon his head until he grew faint and wished to die. For he said, "Death is better than this!"

⁹ And God said to Jonah, "Is it right for you to be angry because the plant died?"

"Yes," Jonah said, "it is; it is right for me to be angry enough to die!"

¹⁰ Then the Lord said, "You feel sorry for yourself when your shelter is destroyed, though you did no work to put it there, and it is, at best, short-lived. ¹¹ And why shouldn't I feel sorry for a great city like Nineveh with its 120,000 people in utter spiritual darkness, and all its cattle?"